"Live your life and have your heart broken once in a while, instead of playing games all the time."
—Cliff Bleszinski, Epic Games

HOW TO GET A JOB IN VIDEO GAMES

Gain the Competitive Advantage to Get
Hired Faster and More Often for Your
Dream Job
OR
The Business of Game Development
and How to Earn a Living in a Creative
Industry
Ken Flemming
MODogma
Austin, Texas

Austin, Texas
MODogma
© 2013 by Ken Flemming.
All rights reserved. Published 2012.
Printed in the United States of America.

ISBN-13: 978-0-9853778-0-9

Library of Congress Control Number: 2012952728

CONTENTS

PREFACE

This book is dedicated to hardworking aspiring game developers who haven't found their breaks yet. This book answers many questions that I had when I began my career, and it answers questions frequently asked by friends who are still struggling to land their first gigs.

I based this book on what I learned in my video game industry experience as an environment artist. I asked questions that people never asked before. My curious nature to find the truth and keep an open mind drove me to compile countless notes from informal discussions with colleagues, leads, and directors.

I asked a colleague—a weathered veteran in the industry—why he hasn't written a book on the subject. He answered, "Are you kidding me? It is so much work!"

The average career of a game developer spans five years. That span *is* increasing, but many people can't handle the pressures and demands the fast-paced industry requires. Game developing interferes with relationships and destroys your health, when you don't manage it properly.

From what I gather, most game industry professionals grow impatient with tedium, and they're accustomed to flourishing. They avoid spending time describing, in understandable terms, what makes them flourish. They don't teach others or detract from time spent improving their skill sets. That's why few professional teachers come directly from the game industry. This book brings their wisdom to light.

Why This Book Wasn't Written Before

While searching for information about the game industry and how it functions, I found a drought. I found vague information online, but I didn't find sophisticated sources offering real insider advice. Authors wrote few books on the subject—authors disconnected from the game industry or lacking writing ability. Existing books about the industry are several years old, and the industry changes dramatically every year.

As an aspiring student, I was fed up with inadequate information. I wanted to learn what studios wanted, so I could prove my value to them. To this day, the lack of game industry exposure is one of my biggest grievances as a developer. Cliff Bleszinski of Epic Games commented that the reason many developers avoid PR (public relations, or interacting with the public, and providing information about the industry) is that "people in the game industry are assholes."

During his speech, "Industry Lessons Learned and Applying Them to the Road Ahead," at GDC 2011 in San Francisco, Bleszinski said the reason that he gained popularity was that "the marketing people found out that there was actually someone at the studio who was good in front of a camera."

I theorize that video gamers just don't care about improving the game industry. They want it to remain a trash-talking, informal society of people living in caves—isolated from the rest of the world. They approve of embarrassing representations of the industry like the *Spike TV Video Game Awards*. They don't want video games to become more prestigious, like the film industry. They're unenthusiastic about teaching other people, because they lack patience and social skills. Thus, professors at game development schools lack the knowledge of experienced developers, because experienced developers don't want to become teachers.

Don't get me wrong, game development schools are essential, and art school *is* the reason I am successful today. However, I'm successful in video games because I figured things out on my own. The problem is that most schools are too easy. Schools don't expect unrivaled students. After all, colleges are businesses. They earn money from enrolled students. Parents justify paying to keep their children in schools when kids perform well, and graduation seems likely. At the expensive private school I attended, the dropout rate was especially high; students couldn't justify paying tuition when they didn't earn adequate grades.

Thus, professors tell students the future is hopeful; they don't push students. These professors are similar to sports coaches, who say, "Don't worry about training too hard, because we *know* we'll win the championship; let's just relax and take it easy."

When I wanted harsher, industry-level critiques of my schoolwork, I requested them outside class. Professors didn't publish written rules about this policy. When the best students got fed up, they ambushed the department chair to request realistic critiques.

Unfortunately, unrealistic criticism doesn't help the bulk of students. Professors shouldn't encourage lazy students to erroneously believe that they're qualified to find jobs. Professors exaggerate the desirability of the game industry to entice students to enroll.

I call this the "*American Idol* Effect," similar to the way candidates are convinced they're talented singers before auditioning, only to discover that they're terrible. People spend their young lives encouraged by parents and peers lacking the guts to provide realistic criticism. In the end, insincere encouragement hurts people more than candor. Someday, that person's heart breaks when she doesn't achieve her dream. Get real with yourself to make progress!

My Early Career

I had a traditional art background. I didn't know how to make it as an artist, but I always daydreamed about working as one. Comic books were my love, so I spent my free time sketching superheroes.

I took an anatomy and physiology class to learn more about how muscles function, so I could draw better heroic figures. Okay, that wasn't the only reason I took the class, but an interest in musculature attracted me, too. Other students in the course were interested in the medical field. They wanted to be doctors or surgeons, but I wanted to follow my passion as an artist.

I followed that passion, despite opposition from people, like my mother, who dearly wanted me to be a doctor. I believed that I could be proficient at anything, when I set my mind to it. My diligence led to a reclusive childhood. I stayed in my room doing homework and drawing, while other kids attended parties and played outside. I missed out on part of my childhood. However, I might have lost focus if I partied and slacked off. Arnold Schwarzenegger said that he was glad that he grew up without television or online social networks, because he wasn't distracted from discovering his chief purpose in life.

I started learning *Autodesk Maya* a mere month before traveling away from home to art school. *Maya* is a 3D art production application that many studios use. I used free tutorial websites such as 3DBuzz.com and DigitalTutors.com to learn the basics of programs that I studied in school. Development schools need the same software that game professionals use at major studios. To determine software studios use, simply review their job listings for your desired discipline.

I learned to manipulate vertices—the basic idea behind 3D modeling—and I created models of characters and cars. During art school, I learned more about *Adobe Photoshop* and *3DS Max*. *3DS Max* is a 3D package similar to *Maya* used by many studios. Studios choose one over the other, so you should learn both.

My first project was seriously terrible compared to the projects of other students in the class. I remained competitive, and I wanted to produce better artwork than everyone else. After class, I researched tutorials online to improve my 3D art.

Someone told me not to compare myself to other students because they lack motivation, and few find jobs immediately after graduation. Instead, I compared my art to that of young employed artists, and then I tried to outperform them.

Contrarily, it's counterproductive to compare yourself to the masters in your prospective field. Competing with masters is daunting, and it convinces you that you aren't progressing as fast as you should. The masters inspire me, but I understand that they did not start their careers at the top.

I also tinkered with *Unreal Editor 3,* a widely used game engine. At the time, *Unreal Editor* wasn't free. I bought a copy of *Unreal 3* to use the editor. The latest editor from Epic, the *Unreal Developers Kit*, is free, and doesn't require game purchase.

I followed online tutorials, and I kept a notepad document for notes about hotkeys and workflow tips. I noted techniques for scripting, visual scripting, adding content, running the game, and more. I recorded troubleshooting information with fixes for problems I encountered. I found little documentation about the editor available to the public, so these notes were my cheat sheets. My notes were particularly useful references when I used the editor after a hiatus and forgot the procedures.

I saved PDF versions of online tutorials, which contained images too complex for text-only documents. Save tutorials and important articles to view offline, because websites hosting the materials might go offline years later, and you'd lose those materials forever. I call the saved resources my *library of tutorials*. Without these resources, I might spend hours finding instructions for minute, forgettable processes, such as the exact settings to bake ambient occlusion in *Maya*.

In school, I was a sponge, learning from professors and top-performing students. Often during group projects, teammates preferred to have fun before a deadline, not caring about their final grades. Instead, I effectively used my time to compensate for their lack of contributions. When I didn't put forth the effort, the project didn't function. At the time, my commitment was a burden. I had to learn processes that weren't part of my job description. However, I now realize that it's smart to learn as much as possible—even learning something you might never use. You never know when that knowledge might help you later.

Because of my hard work, professors recognized my ambition and diligence, and students in my group respected me. I scheduled meetings with professors to discuss my job prospects after graduation. I sought advice about my resume and online portfolio. I researched alumni who found jobs. With this arsenal of knowledge and a spectacular relationship with my instructors, I landed an internship interview prior to graduation.

The internship opportunity came from a professor's former student employed at a startup studio. He conducted a quick phone interview to ensure that I knew *3DS Max*, and to ensure that I'm a likeable guy. Social skills are important in game development, and studios reject candidates who aren't talkative enough. Collaboration is an important aspect of development, and collaboration is impossible without effective communication.

The HR manager called while I was driving fifteen hundred miles to San Francisco for GDC. GDC, Game Developers Conference, is a premier convention for professional game developers to share ideas and career opportunities.

The HR manager scheduled a phone interview with the lead environment artist. I rehearsed a list of relevant questions, preparing to conduct a fluid conversation.

When the lead was scheduled to call me, I waited in a parking lot in Arkansas to give the conversation my full attention.

Interviewing while driving is unsafe, and I didn't want to scramble to find a place to park.

I waited for thirty minutes, but my phone remained as silent as a mouse. Confused and slightly frustrated, I called the HR manager and started introducing myself. She disconnected the call right after I said, "Hello! My name is. . ." Maybe she thought I was a phone solicitor.

I didn't want this opportunity to escape so easily. I called again, and I reached the HR manager's voicemail. I left a message inquiring politely about the call she scheduled with the lead environment artist. I expected her to take days to respond— if she ever did. After my first few attempts with online job applications, I'd learned HR managers in the game industry respond slowly. In my head, I invented reasons the studio didn't contact me.

Disheartened, I drove back to the interstate. Before I passed the first intersection, my phone rang. It was the lead artist. I parked in a nearby lot, and a lengthy conversation ensued. I asked as many questions as I could. I was ecstatic to talk with someone important to my future career. The lead said that he would review the candidates and contact me if he selected me for the internship.

A week later, I began thinking he wouldn't call me back. I was eating lunch on one of the last days of GDC when the HR manager phoned me. She said that I was selected for the internship, and she asked when I could start. I told her I was available in ten days, and she scheduled my starting date, accordingly.

Then, I looked for a place to stay. I met an intern and fellow art school alumni at the studio. He kindly invited me to stay in his apartment while I searched for a room to rent. My original contract was six months long, but the studio extended the contract until the end of the project—eight months total. My contract wasn't converted to full-time employment at the end of my internship because of a hiring freeze. The studio also followed a policy of hiring interns based on seniority, not skill level.

After working for an AAA-game studio, I was ashamed of my portfolio.[1] Completing small tasks during my internship helped me become a faster modeler. My modeling collision improved, and I set up shaders in *3DS Max*. I learned new tricks through trial and error, gained exposure to professionals, received advice from my lead, and asked colleagues to share their wisdom.

I wanted to improve my portfolio with one spectacular piece. The piece took three months of eight-to-ten hour days, five days a week to complete—including time spent posting on forums and iterating based on audience feedback. I tracked my hours in a timesheet when I worked at home. I treated the project like a serious job, although I wasn't paid to do it. I lived frugally, and I stretched my internship savings to pay for my living expenses.

When I applied for jobs, receiving responses took longer than I anticipated—when I received responses at all. Meanwhile, I took an art test. An art test is usually based on a piece of concept artwork that requires modeling and texturing to the set style of the concept and should match the style of the studio giving the test. Art tests are usually required before having an official interview with the lead. Other departments also conduct tests, although they aren't as common as for artists. Nothing came of the test, and I continued searching job listings.

I remembered that an intern at my last job accepted a job with another local studio. He found the available position listed on craigslist.org. I searched on the site and found a quality assurance (QA) position at the same studio. The studio also listed a mid-level environment artist position. With only eight months of experience, I felt unqualified; the listing requested two years. I expected the former intern to recommend me to the studio, but he didn't inform his HR department about my interest in the position.

---

1. AAA games are blockbuster, big-budget games at the top of their classes.

I had to get creative. I attended an art group led by a popular local concept artist. I met an artist working at the studio I whose QA posting I'd found on craigslist.org. We identified our shared interests instantly, and I conveyed my interest in the advertised QA position. He arranged an informal lunch for the QA team and me.

The studio contacted me shortly thereafter to request an interview. Before the interview, I rehearsed my interviewing skills. I nailed the interview, and the studio offered me the job.

My first day, I met an artist who applied for the environment artist position I'd felt unqualified for. He was a college student with *no experience!* His friend working for the studio recommended him. Because he got an interview, I presumed the studio liberally provided opportunities to novices.

In reality, minimum experience requirements aren't set in stone. When you have more advanced skills than your experience on paper reflects, studios make exceptions. Go for it!

I consulted the concept artist who introduced me to the QA team. I invited him to review my portfolio in consideration of the environment artist position. He indicated that my artwork demonstrated that I was qualified for the environment artist position. He recommended that I consult the HR manager. The HR manager promised to share my resume with the art director. A couple of days later, the HR manager scheduled an interview with the art director, and the studio offered me a contract job.

Opportunities exist, and the saying is true that, "it is not important where you start—it's where you finish that counts."

People miss opportunities because they feel they're overqualified for certain positions, they avoid mundane tasks, or they only want their names associated with the biggest studios. Being too picky is a career death wish. It's usually impossible to get into a famous studio when you're new to the line of work. You can pursue your dreams after you acquire experience.

Disclaimer

This book doesn't provide an absolute solution for landing a job; it offers insight into the profession, and it explains which strategies were successful and which failed. Studios differ wildly from one another. This book contains a collection of advice from many game professionals who share their strategies for success.

I wrote this book objectively, including diverse and thorough advice. These techniques get results when used correctly, and they apply to other creative industries—not just video games.

I. PREPARATION

A s a kid, a friend played a joke on me by setting up a reenactment of a popular survival-horror game. I found this unpleasant, and my friend didn't understand why I got upset. This example demonstrates how you should consider perception cautiously, because varying perceptions lead to conflict and frustration during the job application process. Well-managed studios teach classes specifically about mitigating conflicting views of employees, because varying perceptions are prevalent everywhere and affect our daily lives.

Try looking at yourself in the third person, as if you were a bystander witnessing the actions of a complete stranger. Sometimes your audience misses the message you communicate. Generally, exercise respect when you talk with people—particularly when you talk with an HR manager. People notice politeness and professionalism. Manners set you apart when you apply for a job, because your competition in the game industry doesn't always communicate professionally.

1   Saving Money

You might wonder whether saving money is an essential step in the process of finding a job. Many college students blow their savings on tuition and leisurely activities. The money flows when they're hired, right?

In reality, you should maintain a comfortable savings for emergencies. While I attended high school, I saved nearly $15,000 of minimum-wage earnings from my part-time job in a grocery store. The minimum hourly wage then was $5.75. I was not a greedy or needy kid. I didn't want to drive a fancy car or dine in fancy restaurants. I ate at home, lived with my parents, attended school, and enjoyed a "boring" lifestyle. Frugal living is unthinkable for most teenagers. Many Americans spend money with little to show for it later in life. They live on credit, waiting for the next paycheck to pay minimum balances on last month's spending. Living on credit is a vicious cycle, trapping people in unfortunate circumstances.

Instead of borrowing my tuition for an expensive school, I completed my foundation classes at a community college. I appreciated my decision when art school students complained about taking math and other required non-art classes that I had already completed in community college. Like them, I complained about these classes. However, I had paid *much less* for them. After I completed those non-art classes, I was closer to my art school degree. I invested the higher tuition in classes worth taking at an expensive art school.

I used my savings to pay for my college education. My college choices were an expensive art school—which might only be possible with a sizable scholarship—or a local school that wouldn't provide the same life experience or add credibility to my resume. I applied to both schools, and both accepted my applications.

I mentally prepared to attend the less expensive college to avoid accruing excessive debt. Soon thereafter, the expensive art school offered me nearly a full scholarship.[2] I accepted the scholarship without hesitation, and I am proud that I borrowed only a nominal amount of money from my parents (for only one semester). I graduated debt-free! Fellow graduates told horror stories about their debts upwards of $100,000![3]

Let us add up the figures: Graduating and finding an entry-level game-industry position paying $35,000-45,000 annually, you could save about half of your earnings and use the rest to pay for your living expenses. A highly dedicated person with an *aggressive* savings plan might contribute one quarter of her income, after taxes, to repay student loans—or roughly $7,000 annually. She would spend almost fifteen years to repay those debts. Her salary might increase with experience, but her expenses also increase as she ages and accrues more responsibilities—such as a home mortgage, spouse, or kids.

At this book's publication, qualifying for a loan is more difficult than it was when I attended school. Therefore, you're less likely to acquire $100,000 in debt. Future students must plan to save money when they attend expensive schools.

Even financing a mediocre education is difficult without a scholarship to pay a portion of the expenses. The more money you save—instead of spending it on senseless items—the more options you have to attend a school that you can afford.

Ideally, the better the school you attend, the better your chances of employment after graduation. Invest in a school to best help you get a job, which *might not be the most expensive*. Be flexible, so you can afford your preferred school.

---

2. The "portfolio scholarship" covered 75% of the total expenses, and required me to live in the dorms throughout my attendance and maintain a 3.0 GPA, which is fairly easy at most art schools.

3. Well-known universities expect you to spend $90,000–$120,000 on your degree, on average.

The primary criteria defining the "best" game development schools are their proximities to major game developers. This seems like a stupidly simple concept. However, a school's proximity to a major game developer helps you gauge whether or not it places its graduates in jobs. Just like with real estate, it's all about location, location, location!

Examples include the following schools:

- DigiPen in Seattle, near Valve Software
- Gnomon School of Visual Effects in Los Angeles, near Naughty Dog, Inc.
- The Guildhall at SMU in Dallas
- Full Sail University near Orlando

Industry professionals don't travel long distances to provide mentorships; they consort with local campuses. Another advantage of attending a school near a development studio is that industry professionals visit your classes to facilitate tutorials or check your progress. At a school my brother attended, Art Center College of Design in Pasadena, California, professionals visited frequently.

Another resource to determine the best schools in the field is *3D World* magazine. Every year, *3D World* publishes a list of the best digital art schools with its commentary about the selections.

Although the industry might recognize a school, if the school isn't near a major developer you might feel stranded on a barren island. Instead, choose a less prominent school located near development studios—preferably one with industry professionals teaching the courses.

For example, my friend teaches character art classes at a local community college. It isn't a prominent school, yet his students receive better training than students paying top-dollar at well-known schools with washed up professors.

The school I attended is an example of one with a great reputation among unsuspecting high school students. Yet, it's far from the actual game industry. When I attended, professors promised that developers visited classes. However, because of the school's location, actual industry professionals had few opportunities to visit. When professionals did visit, they didn't spend quality time with every student.

In lieu of professional exposure, recruiters advertised their companies and conducted mock interviews. I don't recall a single person for whom an opportunity actually resulted from these interviews. Presumably, studios were unwilling to pay relocation expenses for entry-level students.

Once, an authority figure of BioWare Austin visited the school and lectured about online game design. As a student, I believed he traveled to the school solely to conduct that valuable lecture. I was impressed that our school hosted such a prominent industry figure. I met him years later, and I learned that his main reason for that trip was to visit his family. The lecture was a secondary priority, and it might have justified a tax write-off for business travel.

Sure, all-star students might turn water into wine at inadequate colleges. They might supplement the schools' curricula with their own research. However, relying on research alone defeats the purpose of attending school.

Attending a subpar school makes it harder to obtain skills needed for a job. Avoid wasting your time learning the wrong information, requiring you to re-learn it correctly later. A quote from the documentary about the importance of education, *Waiting for "Superman"* (recommended by Cliff Bleszinski), indicates, "Good schooling is never a bad thing, but bad schooling can become harmful."

Non-accredited schools usually hire former graduates of mediocre colleges who *did not* break into the industry to serve as professors. Thus, self-taught students might find themselves outperforming these professors. Sometimes, student counselors have no more industry connections than students (usually none). Don't waste time and money attending an undesirable school that doesn't benefit your career.

Instead, learn to be autodidactic, or self-taught. Self-teaching is more challenging than holding hands with a professor who guides you through a particular subject—which is why people attend college. But autodidacticism is vastly more rewarding, and it sometimes takes less time than a college education.

Online tutorials—Gnomon School of Visual Effects,[4] *Digital Tutors*,[5] *Eat3D*,[6] and others—can teach what you might learn from a professor. You can rewind and review self-paced videos produced by industry professionals. Two or three five-hour tutorials might take you two weeks to complete, which is equivalent to the lessons you learn in one college course—for a fraction of the time and cost. Many tutorials are even free.

To get started, select a tutorial about a topic that interests you. For example, if you want to become a character artist, try a *ZBrush* tutorial on character sculpting. Follow the tutorial word for word. Don't just watch the video, practice in your own version of the software. You don't acquire martial arts skills watching videos of Kung-fu masters unless you practice your Kung-fu moves!

Software packages usually offer thirty-day free trials or other incentives for students. After you complete a few tutorials, use your new skills to build a project for your portfolio.

As I've suggested in this chapter, the game industry doesn't judge you solely on your resume or degrees. However, degrees earned from accredited schools *do* help programmers—especially during salary negotiation, because it's hard to quantify a programmer's value using lines of code alone. For others, studios expect you to provide an awesome portfolio and stay current with your skills to produce the newest generation of games.

---

4. http://www.thegnomonworkshop.com/
5. http://www.digitaltutors.com
6. http://eat3d.com/training_videos

2   Taming Your Talents: College

College is a subject of hot debate between industry professionals and university professors. Parents usually want their kids to earn proper university degrees, which are encouraging signs of successful futures. Some young people argue that college wastes time and money and doesn't guarantee employment.

The real-world social skills, professionalism, and accountability you acquire earning a university degree are difficult to learn solo. Attending college matures your soul and refines your personality. College might be your first opportunity to define your strengths, weaknesses, and work ethics.

Most aspiring game developers enroll in art and design schools. Aspiring programmers, however, usually attend mainstream universities or technical schools.

If you enroll in an art and design school, prepare for the following:

- **Get used to rich kids.** Children of orthodontists, real estate investors, and TV station owners aren't your competition. Many spend excessive time partying. Considering your level of effort while your peers never lived without a personal butler might be disheartening. The sad reality is that only the wealthy can afford art school without scholarships or debt. Most art schools are privately owned and operated, typically funded by the wealthy—because art school is considered a luxury. Other students slack off (a lot), riding skateboards, watching TV, and playing *Guitar Hero* (or the popular social game at the time)... It's unfair how they have so much fun while you carry the burden of needing a job after graduation. But your diligence will pay off. Granted, rich parents support some of these slackers for their entire lives. You can't change that, so don't let it get you down. Those people rarely contribute much to society, which motivates me to work hard to succeed. I want to give something incredible to the world that no one else provides.

- **New game development programs pop up left and right, but schools don't often cover the essentials.** Community colleges hope to capitalize on the game development craze with flashy advertising and the cunning of tobacco companies marketing candy cigarettes to children. What these schools don't tell you and might not realize, is that they flood an oversaturated job market with unqualified candidates. Standing out is even more difficult, and recommendations are effectively required if you expect a response from a studio. Attend a school with industry connections, email professionals, and attend conferences to build a professional network. Exploit social networking sites such as LinkedIn.com. Your professional contacts are your ticket into the industry, while poorly trained recent graduates desperately approach HR managers in droves.
- **Don't get discouraged.** College is a professional and enlightening experience when you're proactive and bend the rules of the orthodox mentality. (Go to class. Do homework. Sleep. Repeat.)

Defy convention, and seek advice from top professors outside class. Taking initiative to schedule informational interviews helps you get ahead of other classmates, and you learn what it takes to get hired. Professors are more realistic discussing expectations in private discussions than they are when they address entire classrooms. Schedule meetings with your professors during their office hours—professors don't enjoy working weekends any more than students enjoy weekend classes.

College students—especially those attending schools boasting fun curricula, such as video game development—are often spoiled complainers. I suspect that many of these students honestly don't want jobs after graduation. They attend college to appease their parents, who expect college degrees to earn social acceptance. Perhaps these students don't know what to do, so they choose programs that seem fun. Maybe they've enjoyed playing video games throughout high school, and they imagine breezing through college without paying attention or attending class.

College professors are not always forthcoming, because trade secrets aren't shared with everyone. The common unwashed aren't responsible enough to use the information appropriately, so you must earn the right to access the inside scoop.

When you interview professors, they don't share everything about getting into the industry until they're confident that you're a truly hardworking person who deserves such precious insider information. Earn trust by building strong relationships with your professors through hard work and dedication (cliché attributes of success, because they're effective).

Professors boost your reputation around campus when you show enthusiasm by staying after class, learn new principles, and fine-tune your art. Consistently submitting quality work is bound to get attention. Professors influence your future, and they provide references when you apply for your first job. When professors with industry connections admire you, they shepherd you into opportunities, without you even asking.

During informational professor interviews, discuss the following topics:

- Ask about the salaries of previous students. Prepare to negotiate your future salary.
- Ask what types of examples you should include in your portfolio, and ask how you should organize them.
- Request access to online portfolios of former students with successful careers. Their portfolios help you determine the skill level required to entice studios. It is also a good opportunity to earn new alumni contacts.
- Inquire about game-related organizations available outside of class. Join them, and list your affiliations on your resume to show studios that you are committed to your vocation.

College definitely requires more time than teaching yourself. The average bachelor's degree at a four-year university requires you to complete foundation courses for the first two years before you reach the industry-specific courses pertaining to your degree. This is why you should negotiate your own accelerated degree path. If you're already enrolled in a public university, or you're required to complete foundation courses unrelated to the game industry—such as history—*test out* of these classes. You take a test that spans the content of the entire course, which is usually administered by the department chair. By testing out of a particular subject, you demonstrate proficiency and earn credit for the course without spending time learning what you already know. This is also a *huge* money saver!

You can also apply credits based on college-level classes you attended in high school, which might be called Advanced Placement, or AP courses. AP courses save you time and money, and get you to your focus of study sooner to learn techniques for creating video games.

During a lecture presented by professionals at Pixar, a top animator said that when he was in college, it was "uncool" to graduate. Students who made it through college without receiving an irresistible job offer were assumed to lack skills. The best students were whisked away from school to opportunities instead of digging deeper into college debt. Those college students preferred to use their real-world knowledge than to learn in simulated environments.

This might have been true fifteen years ago. Now, it's hard to find a substantive position before graduation. The industry simply has more competition. Software is easier and more intuitive, and applications are available for home use. The lack of jobs in the market unnerves people who've worked hard. My college roommate's sister was casually offered a Nickelodeon internship, and she wasn't even interested in opportunities with Nickelodeon! She landed the internship because she was connected—her parents knew someone at Nickelodeon. Landing a job sometimes requires luck; studios prefer going through direct contacts than hiring someone fresh off the street without a reputation.

3   Researching Your Professors

Another factor you should consider when you decide between autodidactism versus a formal education is how schools lag behind the industry. Even the best colleges' game development programs stay two years behind the current industry standards. Technology constantly changes, and games released today were made with old technology (it was new when they started the game a year or more before). The average game takes two years to produce, and the average lifespan of a game console platform is six years. Every two years, studios change drastically, because they learn while producing every game. Every six years is like a renaissance; studios learn the bounds of new consoles.

To mitigate this constant change, choose a university with professors currently employed in the industry. These professors are hard to find, because employment in the game industry requires more than a full-time commitment. Most developers have no time to teach while they actively work in the industry. The professionals who leave the industry sometimes become complacent, and they fail to study the new technology. Although their knowledge might be more applicable than that of rookie professors, it takes a huge personal effort to keep up with the current pipelines and processes.

Expanding on the notion that professors' knowledge lags behind the industry, *it is not always wise to trust your professors*—particularly at schools that aren't game industry-accredited. This single piece of advice should prove invaluable to you if you're a naïve student who doesn't know what to expect from college. Perhaps you selected your school because of the hype around its relation to the industry, and you wanted to earn good grades. This might seem harmless, but a professor's information is outdated and possibly even wrong.

For instance, a 3D art professor suggested using 4096^2 textures on a 3D vehicle model. This was when the development for *Xbox 360* and *PlayStation 3* had just begun. The professor assumed that technology was so advanced and limitless that game engines could handle this large texture size on a vehicle. Or, he assumed it might work two years later when his students graduated.

If you're unfamiliar with game art, a texture map is a two-dimensional image that represents the surface detail of a three-dimensional object. Texture sizes are measured in square pixels, and each size is doubled. Thus, common texture sizes are 256^2, 512^2, 1024^2, 2048^2, and, very sparingly, 4096^2. Larger textures provide more detail, but they also require more direct memory from the game engine's limited hardware. At this book's publication, games typically use 4096^2 for terrain or large objects that might cover an entire screen. Most games include several art entities onscreen, requiring extensive combined texture memory. Typically, the maximum texture resolution for a vehicle prop should be 2048^2, and vehicles' texture resolutions are usually 1024^2, and 512^2 for open-world games.

Thus, the professor recommended texture sizes four times larger than the appropriate size. If a student shared this inaccuracy with a potential studio during an interview, the studio would immediately be deterred. This inaccuracy might bother studio personnel enough to disregard that student as a potential candidate.

This example illustrates how college professors don't teach you exactly how to meet studios' expectations. Take a professor's advice with a grain of salt, and conduct your own research. Frequent the online forums, and validate information with industry professionals.

When you select a school, research its professors. A telltale sign of inexperienced professors is a lack of previous game industry exposure. Some schools advertise that all their professors are actively employed in their industries, but this might not be true.

The best game development schools appreciate professors with valuable industry connections and compensate them, accordingly. Therefore, tuition for these institutions is steeper than tuition at the most renowned private schools.

Unless you're comfortable accruing a massive amount of debt, you're from a wealthy family, or you earn a scholarship, settle for a college with professors lacking a track record in the industry.

How do you balance cost and quality? Because game industry professionals don't often teach, and private schools are expensive, consider attending a technical school startup. Gnomon School of Visual Effects is the most prominent startup, but other startups are also viable choices.

Startups usually operate in populated cities, such as Los Angeles, where the game industry prevails. Startup schools are informal and usually run by industry veterans. The coursework might not earn you an official degree. You learn the latest techniques quickly, which is advantageous for game developers.

Startup schools are less expensive than private and public universities because they operate independently, without huge overhead costs. Startup schools don't usually offer student housing or transportation systems. Startup instructors provide honest feedback, because they're less concerned with higher-education politics than traditional college professors. Startup schools offer concentrated learning experiences targeted to your success finding a job, without the fluff associated with traditional college.

Bearing in mind the advantages and disadvantages of different types of schools discussed in this chapter, gather a comprehensive list to compare the campuses you're considering. The next page includes a worksheet to assist you.

4   College Campus Comparison

College Name	Degree Length (Years)	Cost Per Year	Total Cost (Degree Length × Cost/Year)	Professors' Qualifications

5   Why College Is Not Always Necessary

Practice doesn't make perfect; *perfect practice* makes perfect. When you practice a task every day for ten years, do you automatically become an expert? **No.** The *quality* of practice is equally important as the practice itself. If you practice keyboard typing daily, but you never look away from the keys, then you continue to hunt-and-peck without learning the key locations or tactile muscle memory required to type efficiently.

Geoff Colvin, author of the successful book *Talent Is Overrated*, calls forced practice *deliberate practice*.[7] Deliberate practice focuses on improving the aspects of a task that you find difficult. Much of this practice involves experimenting or screwing up.

Sometimes you learn a new hotkey or find a better solution accidentally by pressing a particular combination of keys. These Eureka moments only occur when you practice.

If you're a digital artist, custom scripts and tools expedite your workflow. Many custom additions and plug-ins are undocumented, and you need patience to get used to them. However, they add a sizable payoff to your work speed. For designers, write your design ideas in a sketchbook. Programmers, maintain snippets of code to copy and paste. Your code snippet database expands with your experience.

The same goes for sound designers. You can make new sounds with the arsenal of sounds that you created for other projects. Using tools to work efficiently, you might invest one hour of planning to save several hours of execution.

Some learners reach plateaus in their game development skills. As they gain skills, it takes more practice to continue

---

7. Colvin, Geoff. *Talent Is Overrated: What Really Separates World-Class Performers from Everybody Else*. New York: Portfolio Trade, 2010.

growing. Some developers don't push themselves to spend hours at their home computers, especially after long days at the office.

Practice is intrinsically motivating. Instinctively, you practice to improve a certain skill. However, the motivation to practice might be elusive. So, attending school might provide additional motivation to practice.

Elaborating on the idea that perfect practice makes perfect, some scholars believe that mastery requires ten thousand hours of practice—which equates to five years, practicing forty hours per week.

According to the African proverb, "Smooth seas don't create skillful sailors." Expect some failures and challenges along the way. Attempt projects, competitions, and challenges that are more ambitious to expand your talent. In school, especially, when your friends and family suggest you work excessively, you are on the right track!

In his book about game development, the designer known as "Hourences" says it takes at least two to four years to reach an entry-level skill level, working 24/7.[8] Remember that practice should be challenging and innovative; don't just go through the motions.

Practice a new skill for at least one hour daily. When you skip practice one day, recover the lost practice by spending two hours practicing the following day. Practice more when you think you can handle it without overexerting yourself. Practice helps masters continuously improve.

Overtime is an exception. Senior team members and directors admit that they don't practice at home during crunch. Crunch typically means developing over ten hours per day. When developers finish for the day, game development should be the last thing on their minds. Human bodies get exhausted by hours at computer screens. Some developers practice during crunch;

8. Sjoerd "Hourences" De Jong. *The Hows and Whys of the Games Industry.* Antwerp, Belgium: printed by author, 2007.

they usually advance quickly in their careers at the expense of their health or social lives.

College might teach you the user interface of certain applications, but it doesn't make you a proficient user. An artist requires a foundation in art; a designer requires a foundation in design principles, computer science, or psychology; and a programmer requires a foundation in computer science and mathematics. Beauty and fun are subjective, thus they cannot be taught directly but honed through practice.

Only you know how much effort you contribute and how much progress you make. You determine your success. An instructor might help you develop your talent, but only when you're ready to develop it. By openly accepting a professor's advice and applying it in your practice, you develop talent. Instructors don't tell you exactly what to do at every moment. You need internal motivation even when learning from someone else—although arguably less than when being self-taught.

6   Networking

Many aspiring game developers wish the word "networking" didn't pertain to making video games and free-flowing creativity. Networking is often an overlooked opportunity, creating an obstacle between you and your dream job. Many shy developers prefer to gain job qualifications based on pure skill without the social aspect. Don't limit yourself with this perspective.

As the video game industry becomes more accepted and desirable to "normal folk," the personalities in the industry broaden. Personalities of aspiring video game professionals range from partying high-school football players to reclusive nerds locked inside their rooms. Even non-gamers fit into game development—usually in advertising or HR. Traditional gamers have trouble relating to non-gamers, because traditional gamers feel that everyone should share their passion for video games. Welcome to the world of networking, where mere children become true adults!

To get to know someone at the office, address that person by his or her name. A person's name is usually pleasant sounding to his or her ears, and using someone's name shows that you care. Studios usually maintain online resource pages where you can learn the names of your colleagues.

The break room is an effective networking area. When you leave your desk for a snack, water, or restroom break, greet coworkers along your way. Start a little small talk. Especially at larger studios, you might not see colleagues from other departments outside common areas. I've started lasting and beneficial relationships through chance encounters in break areas.

Another way to network is to go out to lunch. To avoid awkwardness, target a group of coworkers who already plan to go out for lunch, and tag along. Yes, brown bagging your lunch might save a little bit of money, but spending time with coworkers might improve your job security and build relationships outside the office. And those relationships lead to future opportunities.

In the game industry, everyone is connected. Some professionals call it a big, incestuous family. So *never* say anything hateful about anyone else. Chances are, you will see that person again during your career. Also, someone you meet at another studio might be a close friend with the victim of your insults.

Consider this ice-breaking conversation as a lesson in avoiding sticky situations that could harm your reputation:

NEW ACQUAINTANCE	Do you know *Person A*?
YOU	Yeah, *Person A* and I used to work together at *Studio X*.
NEW ACQUAINTANCE	What did you think about *Person A*?
YOU	He was okay. *Secretly, you despise him.*
NEW ACQUAINTANCE	Awesome! He's my boyfriend; we met in college.

This example illustrates how to avoid saying something negative in your conversations. Simply recognizing that you know someone is better than extrapolating your opinions about that person—how you didn't like his immature jokes, his roadkill breath, or how he always kissed up to the lead.

Imagine the awkwardness of later discovering that your new acquaintance is closely connected to the person you've just criticized. Odds are, coworkers already know about your bad ties or his roadkill breath without you mentioning them. Don't speak negatively about anyone, unless you're with a close friend you trust. Even then, it's unwise to complain about people. If you speak negatively about colleagues, people assume that you also complain about *them* when they're not around. Instead, remain friendly, and be helpful.

Networking shouldn't happen only at conferences; you have networking opportunities daily on the job that most developers overlook. Getting to know people is important, regardless of your position in life, and too many employees underestimate the benefits of connections. After you get to know others, they feel more open talking with you. They'll cooperate and collaborate with you. Growing studios constantly hire new people. Introduce yourself to new hires, and form relationships with them. When you don't, your circle of influence grows smaller with each new employee entering the studio. Employees with the biggest circles of influence are typically the least dispensable.

Game industry professionals create barriers about the people they talk with, similar to any class-oriented industry. For example, some directors talk only with other directors, avoiding regular employees. Employees talk only with other employees, and they avoid students.

I call a big, fat, steaming pile of B.S. on this one. At networking events, I talk with *everyone*. I start conversations with all conference attendees. You never know whom you will meet or what you can learn from people. Even when you meet people you don't consider valuable members of society—you confirm the sense of the person that you are, noting the type of person you do *not* wish to be.

Being friendly with everyone might be out of your comfort zone—and it is for me, too. But, I psych myself up for the challenge, and great opportunities result. For example, students and industry newcomers ask me to answer provoking questions.

I advise aspiring video game professionals to do your part to make the game industry community stronger with fairness and openness to everyone. You're not too important to talk with people. You were an eager aspiring developer, too. Do you remember how hard it was to approach established veterans in the industry? Wasn't it easier to approach those mavens who were cool enough to share their knowledge? Remembering your own journey should inspire you to spread the good karma at these networking events.

7   Attending Conferences

Bring your communication A game. The first hurdle of speaking with a stranger is hardest to jump. Subsequent encounters get easier. Few new acquaintances approach you and start talking—especially in this industry. In fact, hardly anyone approaches you, so be proactive and initiate a conversation. Otherwise, you'll be standing alone.

Additionally, avoid following familiar people or talking exclusively with your existing friends. It's difficult to meet new people after you satisfy the psychological need to talk with someone. Attend social and networking situations with friends, and occasionally split up to meet new people.

Don't be like a kid sitting at the pool's edge with her feet in the water. She remains afraid of the water until her first leap of courage. Throw yourself into the water, and learn how to swim.

Get into the extrovert mindset. Everyone feels introverted at times. When it comes to conferences and networking opportunities, being affable is the difference between getting a job and staying unemployed. It's the difference between earning a paycheck and living off your parents. It's the difference between realizing your dream and wasting away in self-anguish.

You can practice extroversion by rehearsing in front of a mirror. Practicing also helps you develop effective communication through facial expressions—it's not just a movie gimmick. Another technique is to simulate conversations aloud, and rehearse different scenarios.

Phone a relative you haven't spoken with lately, especially one that you don't know well. Hold a steady conversation for as long as possible. This helps you learn to speak with unfamiliar people.

Initiate conversations in public places such as libraries, in elevators, on buses, or in video game stores. Imagine you are a newborn puppy. Be lively, and show affection to everyone! When you act like a puppy, others match your welcoming attitude. Sometimes, strangers in public settings might respond inappropriately or rudely. However, conference attendees are educated and polite. They don't bite.

Books and pickup artists sell opening lines to get laughs or attention. Simply asking about someone is enough to start a conversation, though. Ask these questions, for example:

- Where are you from?
- What are you doing at this conference?

Aside from asking questions, make conversation by introducing yourself, and then wing it from there. Pickup lines are hard to pull off—even awkward or cheesy—after which, your whole conversation might fall flat. Getting acquainted with people and making contacts is a game of numbers. The more people you meet, the better your chances of meeting someone who can help your career.

I talked with numerous programmers and leads seeking programmers or designers. Our conversations were interesting, but nothing resulted, job-wise. However, I still keep business cards for reference. Have fun getting to know industry professionals and learning about their interests.

I met a man who claimed he created the ever-popular document format Adobe PDF (Portable Document Format). He told me that writing PDF was no big deal, because Adobe paid him to do his job. He claimed he hadn't felt that he made anything revolutionary or extraordinary at the time. Pretty cool! He also noticed that I wore running shoes, which suggested I was a programmer. He shared his theory that programmers don't care about fashion, and they wear running shoes and jeans while other developers wear fashionable dress shoes. If you want to stand out as a programmer, wear jeans with running shoes!

Introduce yourself by approaching someone with your hand extended and face friendly. Say, "Hello, my name is _____. How are you?"

This greeting is particularly useful at conferences, where people move around. You don't have time to conjure up clever lines specific to each person. You might get ignored occasionally, but most people want to talk—especially when they paid to attend a conference to make new contacts.

Another effective technique is targeting people who are standing alone, looking eager. Breaking into conversation groups is difficult, because people might already know each other. The discussion topic might be unfamiliar to you. Still, some social people pick up on the subject of a conversation and boldly jump in. That works too!

Approaching a person standing alone and starting a conversation allows you to be less rushed and more personal than joining into a group conversation. Also, a one-on-one conversation is more likely to lead to a permanent contact.

Be humble when you talk with game developers at conferences; don't be arrogant. Being humble might seem self-explanatory, but people avoid developers with cocky walking styles or flashy looks.

Most experienced professionals don't share insider information. Recall that game developers are introverted; they're not particularly social, so it takes time for them to open up. Often, game developers resort to drinking alcohol at parties to loosen up. Alcohol fights inhibitions and keeps you relaxed when you approach people, when you are above the drinking age. Event planners often provide free alcohol. Good etiquette suggests that you should only consume one or two drinks in a business situation.

Avoid making a fool of yourself. In the game industry, I've observed ultra-intoxicated conversations about immature and embarrassing subjects. Most people don't seem to mind, though, and sometimes drunk people benefit from the additional attention. I don't recommend you get *that* drunk, because your conversations become less productive.

Shy people find it awkward to converse with strangers, but I've participated in many awkward conversations; they can actually be fun! When someone continues to stand near you, he or she remains interested in talking. The conversation might begin roughly and end up being fascinating. Treat these approaches as a private game; determine how many people you meet or how many business cards you can collect in one evening.

Force yourself out of your comfort zone, and talk with a superstar. You might face a rare opportunity to speak with a leading figure of importance in the game industry. Attend a lecture conducted by one of your idols. Then ask her a question after the lecture. You might get nervous, but people who approach their idols and create opportunities are the people who face their fears. They figure, "If I'm this nervous either way, I might as well do it!"

Nothing starts a good conversation and separates you from the sea of average prospective employees like a thought-provoking question. Experienced public figures are accustomed to answering the same boring questions repeatedly. A cliché question leads to a cliché response, which doesn't provide new information.

Avoid the following cliché questions:

- How do you like working for studio X?
- What is your favorite video game?
- How many people does your studio employ?

A thought-provoking question takes longer to answer, and you might learn more than you expect. The speaker tailors a response to your question. Which conversation do you prefer?

Thought-provoking questions include the following:

- Do colleagues at your studio socialize outside the office?
- What are popular activities that employees enjoy together?
- What is the most engaging task you completed recently?
- Do game development studios prefer to hire employees who stay at one studio for years or candidates who switch studios frequently?

Cliff Bleszinski answered the last question, indicating that studios prefer candidates who build long-term reputations at studios to "jumpers." Constantly switching studios suggests that an employee won't stay long enough when a studio hires them.

Information is worth more than gold, and you might learn something that changes your life—when you ask the right questions.

Some people speak with different accents or lack English fluency. Others might not know what to talk about. When you pause to allow time for a response, people usually start talking about *something*. No person's life is so uneventful that she doesn't have a single thing to say. When you introduce yourself to someone who turns her head away in disinterest, respect her poor social habits, and blow past her. Don't let the rude habits of others impact your mojo. Proceed to the next person, and introduce yourself with the same energy as though the night is still young!

When you attend a video game conference, expect a casual, informal atmosphere. Game developer personalities are excruciatingly critical, so grow thick skin. Don't take their comments too seriously. Developers also have naturally laid-back attitudes. Don't expect a strictly business conversation wearing a coat and tie affecting perfect grammar. People want to be treated as friends, and they're open to funny, interesting, crude, and geeky colloquy.

I overheard a story from a major studio's HR representative at GDC in 2011. She explained the importance of social skills to an expo organizer. She said that a student approached her and said only, "Here's my resume for game design."

The student departed without saying, "Hello," or, "How are you?"

The HR representative promptly discarded the student's resume. If you think that the game industry consists of cowards who don't talk much, take note that times are changing, drastically. HR managers know little about games or how to make them. They *do* understand social dynamics, read body language, and determine who is a genuine candidate.

Speak a common language to stand out. When the HR employee returns to the office, managers ask her, "Is this person respectful and enthusiastic enough to fit in here?"

When an HR manager thinks you're not a good fit, she might prevent you from talking with the developers.

Studios hire social people, because HR managers deal with enough problems stemming from poor communication between the non-social people *already employed* in the industry.

Another strategy to get face-to-face time with developers at a studio is to ask a friend who already works for the studio to recommend you. Your friend slices through the networking process and puts you right into an interview.

Handle yourself appropriately, and speak properly and charismatically. But don't limit yourself to the studios where you know people, because many college students don't have industry contacts before they graduate. To access big studios—including your dream studio—you must deal with strangers. In today's game industry, you need social skills!

Conferences are expensive. To mitigate the cost, *volunteer*. By volunteering at a conference, you get familiar with the territory. Many volunteers work in game studios, and they are a social subset of the industry. Volunteers develop connections that lead to job offers. At conferences, it is less important to be at the right place at the right time, but to *be with the right people*.

Another benefit to volunteering is having the opportunity to acquire new friends and contacts. However, don't forget that your first mission is to meet game developers. Some volunteers stay in their comfort zones among other volunteers during conferences, and they miss the magic that game development offers.

Attend sessions and lectures, particularly career seminars. Ask numerous questions. The game industry remains relatively small, so you might see the same people at future conferences. I highly recommend joining the CA (conference attendee) program for GDC San Francisco. Tim Bringle and Ian

Mackenzie lead the program, and they enjoy sharing their experiences with newcomers.

Consider joining meet-up groups to practice your social skills (Meetup.com). Find industry-related groups in your area. Groups allow improvised conversations, and joining groups might lead to job opportunities—depending on the connections of your group members.

For instance, a group of artists used to meet in a coffee shop to sketch artwork and discuss the field. This artists' group wasn't a competitive environment, and it allowed people to practice weekly without the loneliness of working at home alone. Watch out, because some group leaders allow only employed game industry professionals to participate. Exclusive groups don't help you find a job unless you have one already.

Some industry professionals can't share industry knowledge with people lacking signed NDAs (non-disclosure agreements).[9] You might not encounter such "invite-only" groups until a video game studio hires you.

When you attend lectures, don't sit alone. Find a good seat before a lecture. Sitting near others contradicts the natural shyness of game developers. Some people prefer to sit in the back to keep distance from people. I find that sitting right next to someone encourages him or her to talk with you. Nobody likes an awkward silence. When you start a conversation, it's hard for people to run away—especially when they sit right next to you in a small room. Talking with people is easier when you have a gadget to serve as a conversation starter. Demonstrating a new phone game or sharing a video related to the conference sparks quick interest.

Using this technique, I met a producer for Remedy Entertainment. He worked on *Alan Wake* before its release. He

---

9. A non-disclosure agreement is a legally binding document between an employee and a studio dictating that the employee must not share proprietary information. Studios protect their IP (intellectual property—the brands and characters).

requested a thoughtful game review after I exhibited my interest. You don't enjoy interesting interactions until you leave your comfort zone and sit near a stranger!

8   Staying Motivated

My uncle says, "Working out at the gym is fun at first, but it gets old fast." His motivation to exercise resembles the motivation of most mid- to senior-level game studio employees.

My uncle's beer gut is evidence of his lost figure. Would you admit, "Getting rich is fun at first, but it gets old fast?"

People find it unfathomable, but people with money often don't enjoy life as they anticipated. Jaded veterans of the game industry share the predicament. They're familiar with a profession they used to value, and now they take it for granted.

The game industry is not all fun and games. You do enjoy exciting times finalizing projects. More often, serious developers and rockstars in the industry strive to constantly improve, completing personal projects during their free time. They don't play the latest and greatest video game or watch a hot television series marathon. People expect life in a big funhouse as seen in the movie *Grandma's Boy*. The movie portrayed constant camaraderie at the office, but it never showed the game developer *working*.

During a 2011 lecture, a Pixar producer said that Pixar's visitors and new employees expected the most entertaining job in the world. Employees' desks decorated with action figures and Christmas lights perpetuated this illusion of jocularity. When you pay close attention, you see that those employees do actual *work*—and much of it. People put fun objects in their workspaces to relieve stress, to deal with pressure, and to remind them why they do what they do—to provide fun for others.

Numerous studies reveal that money and fame aren't the best motivators, because these motivators are shallow and unrelated to one's true needs. When you focus on the person you want to become—which talents and personality traits you want to possess, places you want to visit, or people you want to meet—you are motivated to be successful. Serious goals provide more ammo to maintain your momentum. When you contribute to projects that you're passionate about, time escapes you. You're personally committed to creating or finishing a project or solving a problem, and you take pride in the result.

To tackle a long-term goal, divide it into smaller, digestible pieces. If your goal is to enter the video game industry, and you're unemployed or working part time, contribute forty hours a week to creating art, designing, or programming for a modern game engine.

If you choose a larger project—an entire game level, for instance—divide it into parts. First, design the level, and then create the art. Divide the level design into sequences players encounter, placement of enemies and props, and in-game mock cinematics. Divide the artwork into individual props, populating the level. Place your props in the environment, and then fine-tune textures and materials.

When you finish a large project, you'll ask yourself, "How did I create all that?"

One piece at a time.

In an article about the level-building process in *Crysis* by Crytek, a lead designer said that Crytek's plans on paper rarely match the execution.[10] Crytek makes art props, and developers place them in games. Crytek continues the design in the actual game engine. This process is called *iterative design*, which is a faster method to create games. The mantra is, "Get it in game, and get it in early."

When developers have content in game, they determine how it functions. Starting a project motivates you to continue working on it until you complete the project. When you plan ad nauseam without executing, you convince yourself that your goal is too lofty or too time-consuming.

Iterative design doesn't suggest that conventional planning is ineffective. Iterative design is a trial-and-error style of design. Developers constantly refine a design based on new discoveries or testing. Often, conventional design is stronger

---

10. *3D World* magazine, 2009.

because of its basis on a good foundation. But, problems arise when the theorizing phase of design lasts too long, and the design doesn't comply with the engine's constraints. When an overall idea about a level is more quickly thought out, relatively speaking, designers are forced to test the mechanics in game, and refine on the fly. The results usually turn out better than heavily preplanned designs that aren't tested in game. Starting in game sparks creativity, too, when designers experience writers' block.

In a conversation with Cliff Bleszinski, I asked whether Bleszinski anticipated his fame early in his career. He said that he was more egotistical during his youth, and he planned to become something big. This is a common theme among great people. Movie stars and musicians anticipated their success and created visions of their potential. They don't land there without aiming. With motivation and confidence, you can do anything. You must learn and practice, but motivation and confidence keep you going through the harder aspects of learning a talent. Some successful people are *over*confident. Don't confuse overconfidence with narcissism. Even those who don't publicly display their egotism have strong self-esteem. Don't hesitate to become the best in your field and compete internationally. You will surely encounter opposition. The higher you aim, the more opposition you face. But, opposition doesn't stop the current titleholders.

Avoid the negative aspects of overconfidence, such as considering others to be inferior. Publicly insulting a colleague's skills damages your reputation. Professionals play for keeps. Unfair criticism is rude—even when people lack skill. Openly expressing your egotism is boasting—a turnoff to everybody else. Be humble; don't publicly broadcast your confidence. Being humble doesn't mean you *lack* confidence; it means you keep it to yourself, and let your work speak for you. You team with others and impart credit for their contributions.

If you're an unemployed college graduate unmotivated to do anything with your life, consider this advice from a seasoned artist in the industry. He said that he was laid off from his game development job. Most developers are unemployed at some point.

During his downtime, he worked for an oil manufacturer on an ocean rig. The job was physically demanding, required long hours, and his team stood in waist-high water repairing broken pipes. His experience resembled an episode of *Dirty Jobs*. He said that his dirty job "really put a fire under his ass," meaning it gave him a burning desire to avoid such unfulfilling and physically demanding labor. The backbreaking conditions motivated him to return to the game industry.

Unfortunately, few people interested in video game careers who attend expensive schools experience such a rude awakening. Heck, most applicants for game-industry jobs have never worked legitimate jobs. It's no wonder people in the industry don't appreciate their jobs, even early in their careers, when their futures seem promising.

9   Staying Awake (Without Coffee or Adderall)

College taught me a great lesson about focus. Procrastination is a pitfall of many college students. When I wanted to get work done for a project on a tight deadline, I stayed awake later than usual. Over time, I learned to manage my time better to avoid sleep deprivation. But starting out, I was too laid back—even after being considered a nerd in high school. I had to whip myself into shape.

My technique was to lie down on my bed, slowly counting to a specific number in my head. I opened my eyes when I reached that number, forcing myself to wake up at that moment. Sometimes I was too tired, and I fell asleep. Usually, when a project was due within the next day or two, I awoke without a problem. My magic number started at fifty. When I wanted more relaxation, I'd count to one hundred. This strategy got me through the night, and I'd eventually catch my second wind.

I am proud that I only pulled two or three all-nighters throughout my entire college career. Other students bragged about how little they slept the night before a project deadline. Their lack of sleep was evidence of their poor time-management skills. These students were too busy partying to do their schoolwork. Because they procrastinated, and there are only so many hours in the last night before class, their projects were less than 60% complete, tops. Not much to brag about, is it?

When you're tired, try to wake yourself by walking. Walking allows gravity to pump blood through your body, and it fires up your muscles and neurons. A walk is better than a nap. Walking usually doesn't cause trouble for workflow, because walking doesn't keep you from your computer for as long as a nap.

Some people drink caffeine or other energy supplements to stay awake. First, it is strange that people drink coffee in the morning after they stroll into the office at ten a.m. Secondly, coffee—and energy supplements, especially—provide only a quick fix. Staying active and stimulating your brain with new thoughts or new scenery are far healthier ways to stay awake.[11]

---

11. "Stand Up, Walk Around, Even Just For '20 Minutes'." NPR.org: May 2012.

10 Knowing What You Want

"Focus on the top end and let the bottom end take care of itself."
–Donald Trump

Focus on what you do well, and do that, and your strengths outshine your weaknesses. Hideo Kojima doesn't need to be a good chef, but he is one heck of a game designer. There are too many distractions and interesting topics in this world to excel at all of them—especially in our modern microwave society, with generic entertainment and advertising hitting spectators in the face constantly. These fads live short lifespans, because they're produced quickly and not designed to last. Humans have everything readily available, making it harder to cut through all the noise to formulate a success strategy. Bruce Lee, the legendary martial arts and philosophical master, put it best when he said, "The successful warrior is the average man, with laser-like focus."

Do not underestimate the importance of high self-esteem. If you don't have it, do yourself an invaluable favor by learning how to develop and practice this characteristic. Nobody knows your true potential better than you do, and nobody takes better care of you. Have faith in yourself, and believe that you can do anything. When you continually strive to achieve a goal, you eventually achieve it.

Many of my friends from school didn't find jobs for months or years after graduation. They persevered, though, and eventually became successful. Finding a job might take one or two years, but it feels like no time in the grand scheme of life. People less confident about making it surrendered and sought other careers. You only go as far as your mind allows you, and you determine this by how high you aim, what you expect from yourself, and your confidence to meet those expectations. Set personal goals, and expect more from yourself when achieving them. When you offer something completely different from everyone else, the spotlight shines on you!

Success can strike unexpectedly, but it's always conceived beforehand. It takes focused discipline. I've heard numerous stories about game developers who built levels as a hobby and didn't expect to actually make a career out of game design. Those days are long gone. The game industry is more serious; barriers to entry are higher. Expectations for job candidates grow seemingly limitless. Sure, indie developers have informal job requirements that are easier to break into. But, people hired by the best studios work their butts off on mods and personal projects instead of casually practicing in their spare time, just for fun.

The students who find jobs after graduation diligently fine-tune their talents for their chosen careers. In some entertainment careers, faking a way to success works effectively. For example, rappers sing about affluent lifestyles, and the public loves it. Some aspiring rappers had little money to sing about, yet made it seem as though they had it good. They later earned bundles selling albums.

Other careers, game development included, require the opposite strategy: You need the skills to rival professionals *before* you get hired. When a studio hires you, you should already feel as though you *are* an actual developer. "Fake it 'til you make it" does not apply here!

11   The Changing Game Industry

The recently sparse job market is evidence of increasing competition in the game industry. Starting out now requires an intense drive and planning. A random, yet surprisingly wise, man at a gas station asked me, when I told him about my impending graduation, "Why video games? Those creative industries are already oversaturated."

He was right, *oversaturated* is the perfect word to describe creative industries. The supply of applicants far exceeds the actual demand for them. Studios have the luxury of choosing the top performers. To filter the applicants, most game studios require a bachelor's degree from an accredited four-year university. This was not the case five years ago, during development for *PlayStation 2* and *Xbox*.

How do you get a recommendation as a student? You might get lucky and find a schoolmate hired at a studio, or your friend might know people who can get you a job. The chain continues, and you may end up getting a referral from a friend of a friend of a friend. You might be lucky enough to have a relative who can get you in. If this is the case, do us all a favor, and actually put in the time to be good at what you do. Many employees in the corporate world find cushy positions based on their relationships, yet they are embarrassments to their studios, and they lower moral.

Nepotism exists in all industries. Thankfully, most game industry professionals pull their weight to stay continuously employed. The fast-paced game industry requires mastery. At a startup AAA studio, a top director gave his younger brother VIP treatment. The studio paid his younger brother's tuition at a renowned art college. His younger brother associated with the studio's industry veterans, and the studio seated him near the top performers.

Although it's tough to swallow, the film industry's interest might lead to a convergence with the game industry. Talented filmmakers covet the stability of the video games, increasing applicants in the oversaturated game industry. Don't be deterred; popular industries get saturated. Great game professionals continue to find jobs.

12   Staying Fit

"A section about physical health in a book about making video games? You're kidding me, right? Why must I be physically fit in the video game industry? Isn't the game industry the only place I can be out of shape and not have to worry?"

This is the *exact* reason that people should consider their health. Many people in the industry don't take care of their bodies and consider poor health normal. They set a bad influence and give the industry a bad name. They attribute poor health to the job, which requires sedentary activity. It's true, sitting on your butt all day doesn't enhance your six-pack abs.

Consider, though, how many other industries involve sitting at desks, yet those people seem healthier than those in the game industry. The shape of game industry professionals results from a diet of pizza, energy drinks, and staying awake too late as an accepted lifestyle. This is changing, and people who care about their health are moving to the industry.

An advantage to good health is that your mind is more receptive to learning, and your brain acts quicker to solve problems. Plus, your body has more energy throughout the day. Just the feeling of being fit is great, and gives you a more positive outlook on life.

I should know; I was over forty pounds overweight as a child. I made the change to a healthy lifestyle. I want to be a positive influence for the game industry, and I set the example that it is possible to be a full-time employee and stay healthy with an active social life. This section describes how to be successful in video games while you enjoy physical activity on the side.

Opinions vary about adequate sleep. Young people often stay awake at night partying and attempt to work the next day. Sleep should not be overlooked for its important benefits. First, sleep deprivation causes your sluggish brain to make mistakes. Sitting in an office chair doesn't stimulate your body, either, making it easier to feel the urge to fall asleep when you're tired. An office chair is almost as comfortable as a warm bed. When you don't burn calories, your body and mind get tired. Your heart works harder than it should.[12] Does that make employees happy?

Savvy studios discourage excessively long days. Studios receive diminishing returns from employees after peak performance. Walking helps you stay awake. However, when your tired body direly requires sleep, walking doesn't help regain your lost energy. A rechargeable battery can work only as hard as the level of charging that it received. The same goes for humans. We must recharge every night to prepare for the energy we expend the next day. There is no substitute for sufficient sleep.

Another mistake many game developers make is eating an improper diet in the workplace. Many studios provide junk food and candy for snacks, because junk is easier to preserve in vending machines. On top of that, some seemingly "healthy" foods are actually not that great. It's tempting to dine out for a tasty lunch and consume large portions of food. Excess food and heavy calories require energy to digest, leading to a post-lunch slump.

The post-lunch slump leads you to drink extra caffeine, over-stimulating your heart. Studios provide energy bars for developers to alleviate their low energy symptoms. However, those bars are intended for endurance athletes doing lengthy exercises, and for camping excursions where food is not readily available. Energy bars contain many carbohydrates, and carbohydrates turn into fat when you don't burn them off with strenuous activity. Personal trainers support the notion that "carbohydrates are evil." Most eaters avoid trans-fat and saturated fat. Carbohydrates are equally dangerous, yet they rarely make the spotlight.

Exercising is necessary throughout the day, even just a minimal amount. Hip exercises are important for people with desk jobs, because excessive sitting leads to over-tightening your hip flexors—the Tensor Fascia Latte (TFL). I am a healthy

---

12. Klosowski, Thorin. "How Sitting All Day Is Damaging Your Body and How You Can Counteract It." Lifehacker.com: Jan 26, 2012.

person, yet I required a chiropractor's care after I injured my back at the gym. The injury was the result of weak hip flexors from sitting. Your hips affect your posture, and you need hip strength for perfect form in exercises such as squats.

People risk developing sciatica—rupturing the sciatic nerve—from excessive sitting. Sciatica treatment requires using a specialized chair to reduce the strain from the hamstrings and direct weight to your knees to alleviate pain. Not fun, and not cheap. The condition is treatable, but you should avoid losing control of your body from excessive sitting.

Another important exercise for people with desk jobs is the hand stretch. Hand stretches protect against carpal tunnel syndrome. Stick your fingers out straight. Bend them away from your palm with your other hand, so that they bend backward. Hold this position for twenty seconds. Do this to both hands. Do hand stretches before you type on the keyboard or grasp the mouse, because your hands tend to stay in the closed position and tighten, which makes typing a burden.

Home workout programs, like P90X, provide a blatant answer to sedentary lifestyles. Use these programs to combat the sedentary workplace experience, and give your body the natural exercise that it requires. Video programs such as these take thirty minutes to an hour to complete, you can do them at home, and they're effective when you do them every other day. The hardest part is turning on the video. The exercises are paced for various intensity levels, and viewers can take breaks and exert the effort comfortable for them.

The correct sitting position is important for your posture. The science of positioning your body is called *ergonomics*, and some studios provide training to help employees practice healthy ergonomics. When you sit, keep your back straight and your chest out. Slumping is bad for mobility and can lead to stiff back muscles. You can find videos and classes about positioning your chair correctly. Some people shrug off these precautionary measures, but they are important for a reason; maintaining a strong, healthy posture is more important than feeling comfortable in your chair. When you feel discomfort from sitting constantly, get up. Take a walking break to loosen your body, and get your blood flowing. Also, prevent yourself from crossing your legs or leaning too far back in your seat.

Nighttime eye drops are necessary for computer users, especially for corrective lens wearers. Optometrists report cases of strained eyes from technology industries because of dryness. Staring at a computer all day causes your eyes to blink less, which dries them out. Dry eyes cause straining and twitching, and dryness has adverse effects on your vision. Using one to two drops of tear-simulated formula in each eye before bed at night prevents dryness. Don't use more, because your eyes risk dependency on the virtual tears and might stop producing enough tears on their own.

13   Publishing Your Portfolio

Your portfolio is perhaps the most important factor in landing a job. Your portfolio should include the following components to meet industry-expected standards:

- **Demo reel:** Include one to two minutes of your best work, with a maximum of thirty seconds per object/piece. Common formats include .avi and .mov at 640 × 480 resolution. I recommend you include multiple formats, because some people use Macs and some people use PCs, and they're unwilling to spend the time to resolve a video problem when they must review other candidates, also.

- **Images:** Include ten to twenty screenshots of your best projects. Organize them with your strongest images first. Your portfolio is only as strong as your weakest examples; don't include anything you're even remotely uncomfortable sharing. It is better to cut something you are unsure about instead of keeping it in your portfolio. Students might hesitate to cut pieces left and right, because they don't have large portfolios to begin with. An art director from Raven Entertainment Software, Inc. said that you unofficially approve the content on your portfolio website when you post it there. Thus, weak pieces in your portfolio indicate your inability to differentiate strong pieces from weak ones.

- Take all your screenshots in a game engine. Previous game engines couldn't simulate complex lighting calculations or generate high-resolution textures or record in-game videos. Pre-rendering an image without using a game engine is now considered dishonest. Typical professional portfolios include screenshots of gameplay designs and 3D models in a game engine. For artists, include wireframe overlays and show objects from multiple angles. Also, some reviewers no longer appreciate turntables to show single models and props, because turntables are cliché.

It is more stylish to do a three-quarter camera sweep, for each side of the model.

- New, intuitive tools for creating games allow users to reveal their full imagination without being restricted by the software limitations. With *ZBrush, Unreal Developers Kit,* and other cutting-edge real-time software, you have no excuse to publish less-than-phenomenal examples. Be proud of your games, because now the art looks as good as the movies, and the design plays just like a professional AAA title!

Target your favorite studio with your portfolio. If you want an environment artist job at a studio, create modular buildings in the studio's style within its budget. The same goes for design or programming. Find a design or system compatible with a studio's games in production. FPSs, MMOs, and platformers require completely different mechanics designed according to the type of game.[13] When you mimic the styles and mechanics of the best studios, you appeal to smaller studios striving to keep pace with the big ones. For example, most MMO studios aspire to compete with Blizzard Entertainment. By creating art or design in Blizzard's style, it automatically appeals to smaller studios producing MMOs.

Technological advancements directly affect job descriptions. Jobs grow more specialized, and you should collaborate with a team on your portfolio instead of going at it solo so you can create an improved showpiece. When you display the piece in your portfolio, highlight your contributions. Reviewers understand when your examples aren't completely your own—they care about the final product's quality.

---

13. FPS is first-person shooter, MMO is massive multiplayer online, and platformer is a style of video game with open-world format jumping obstacles.

14   Critiquing Your Work

Learn to be your own harshest critic. When you experience a formal critique, you feel less delicate. Develop an eye for finding fault in your own work, and fix the major problems before others notice. Furthermore, take the advice, revise, and return with a new and improved product. Feedback helps you improve, so consider creative opinions. With this frame of mind, you don't feel threatened by comments about your work. Be thankful, and give people credit for helping you improve.

Seek advice from those in similar disciplines—especially those who are more talented or experienced. Avoid soliciting opinions from novices or the untrained public, because they don't know what is right and wrong, and they might send you in the wrong direction. Sometimes, you should seek opinions from the public. The public can help you determine whether your game is likable, functional, and understandable for average people. When you want to improve, though, ask people with more experience or talent than yourself. When you receive criticism from untrained reviewers, do not be aggressive when their views conflict with yours. Share your appreciation for their opinions, and simply disregard the advice. Sometimes, you receive helpful feedback from untrained critics, too, so don't be closed-minded. When you receive your critiques, evaluate the feedback. When you see a pattern in the criticism, make it your top priority to implement the appropriate changes.

15 Avoiding Cliche

If you are an artist, cars, space marines, medieval cathedrals, and scantily clad women with big boobs are all played out. If you are a designer, another Mario or Pac-Man mod might get you noticed, but probably not for too long. Contrarily, zombie mods are extremely popular, and they never seem to get old. Go figure! To grab attention, you should be creative, and devise something the public hasn't seen yet. Even when your game isn't beautiful, technically, it might have more merit with a well-executed idea. Trying something new, or doing something old with a new twist, is better than regurgitating what was formerly popular.

16 Using Shortcuts

An art teacher in high school engrained into my mindset that
creating art that directly mimics photographs is cheating, and
you should craft true art by live observation or memory. The truth
is, you aren't cheating by using photo textures or modeling an
object based on something in real life. Most professionals do the
same thing. Achieving photo-realism in a game requires
photographed textures. Even traditional art schools and
professional artists draw from photo references. Also, people
essentially copy from each other, so it may be faster to elaborate
on an existing idea, instead of creating a new one from scratch.
Take the iPhone and its subsequent imitators, for example. It
doesn't hurt to copy bits of an artwork or design, as long as you
do something new with it and make it cool.

II. FINDING A JOB

1   Applying for Jobs

Your application is your fundamental calling card to communicate your qualifications to studios. The format should follow the same standards HR employees are accustomed to reading, because they review many applications and don't want to decipher an application that tries to break the mold.

Include the following components with your application:

- **Introduction email:** Your email should be about two sentences long. Get straight to the point. Include your background information in your cover letter and resume, which you attach to the email.
- **Cover letter:** Your cover letter should be about five sentences long, or one paragraph.
- **Resume:** Your resume should be one page long.
- **Web address to your portfolio:** Include a hyperlink that directs the recipient directly to your portfolio homepage.
- **Follow-up email:** One to two weeks after you send the introduction email and application, send a follow-up email.

2   Writing a Cover Letter

Limit your cover letter to one page. A standard cover letter is about three paragraphs long, and it outlines your previous experience and the lessons you learned from each position.

Your cover letter also explains why you are a good fit for the studio, and it lists your contact information. Some students wonder whether a cover letter is necessary. Cover letters are *not always* necessary, but it is better to include one. When two similar candidates apply to a job with similar credentials, a cover letter might decide who gets hired.

Your cover letter should reference only recent job experience, and preferably only game-industry experience. When that's impossible, describe how your previous job's required skills are useful for a job in video games. You can find tons of resources online describing how to write a cover letter. For examples, check out www.QuintCareers.com.

3   Writing Your Resume

If your portfolio is the brain of your application, then your resume is the heart. The resume is the driving foundation telling potential employers that you have what it takes to handle the expectations at their studios. Your resume should be one page long, formatted for *Word* or PDF—although flashy PDFs with graphics and collapsed/rasterized text aren't as useful to companies as a basic and well-organized *Word* document.

First, it is easier to update new experience to a *Word* document. Secondly, studios and HR representatives use digital copies of your resume in an auto-filing system. These systems check the format of your resume and transfer information to an online database. Studios keep your resume on file for future reference. When you collapse text into a single image, the system can't input the information. Thirdly, make your resume easy to read, and make the content easy to find. If you want to use your resume as a means to stand out, then make it as clean and professional as possible, instead of over-crowding it with eye-catching visuals or multiple custom fonts. The cover letter, not the resume, should be the more creative part of the application, and it can include images or a different style of formatting.

4   Emailing HR Representatives

When you are just starting out, and you don't know whom you should email at a certain studio, email a generic *jobs@studioX.com* address, or complete an online application for that studio. When you find the email address of a HR representative, it is better to email him or her directly. Sometimes you can find an HR representative's email address using LinkedIn.com. Do a corporation search for the studio name, and narrow the list of employees down to the HR manager.

It's even more effective when you know someone at the studio, because you can request the HR manager's contact information.

The most effective way to get into a studio is through a referral. When a friend is familiar with your experience and has a job at the studio where you'd like to work, contact your friend and ask for a recommendation.

Recommendations are treasured currency based on trust. Don't be surprised when your acquaintance is uncomfortable giving you a referral if she hasn't worked with you much, or if she doesn't feel that your skills are strong enough yet. By giving a referral, she's saying that she approves of you and your talent. She's sacrificing her reputation based on your performance.

When you consider recommendations from this perspective, it is no wonder that referrals are *supposed to be* difficult to get. Some professionals hand out referrals liberally, or they recommend people based on friend status instead of merit. This adds untalented people to the industry, when talented recent graduates would better fill the positions but have a harder time getting hired. Please use careful consideration when someone requests a referral, because inadequate new hires slip through the cracks when you don't. Technically, managers are supposed to screen candidates to determine whether they will indeed be good hires. However, at smaller studios, a manager might not be very good at judging candidates' potential during interviews.

Get used to rejection. When you don't get rejected left and right, then you are doing something wrong or you are super lucky. Rejection is natural. The larger the audience, the more rejection you face. Baseball players who score the most home runs are also the ones who strike out the most at bat, because they continue to put themselves at the plate.[14] You must get used to risk and be willing to fail, despite rejections. Not all fish bite, but one fish bites when you keep out your lure.

Some HR departments don't respond to applications. A normal response to an application might take up to two weeks.

---

14. Tony Robbins coined this analogy referring to Babe Ruth being the best home run hitter and MLB players with the most strikeouts.

5   Communicating With Studios

Usually, when a studio responds, the first email indicates only the studio's name as the point of contact in the email closing. When the studio wants more information about you, its HR representative provides the studio name and his or her name in the second email. When the conversation progresses further, he or she sends an email including the studio's name plus its phone number, fax number, physical address, and the name of the producer's first-born child (kidding). The studio develops trust when they get a sense of your personality and talk with you more.

Develop open relationships with studios. Inquire about a studio's processes, and ask what they seek in a candidate. You should conduct this research several years before you graduate. That way, you have more information to guide your school projects, and you don't appear desperate to the HR representatives. HR managers typically give more genuine information to students than recent graduates who need jobs soon, because they know that students have time to heed their advice.

These informal conversations help HR representatives remember you, and they'll respond faster to your emails when you actually apply for jobs. Be polite to everyone at the studio, receptionist included, whether on the phone or through email— even when you get rejected. Typically, everyone you meet at a studio shares opinions about you with the hiring manager. You represent yourself through your behavior, and you shouldn't limit your future opportunities over something silly, such as getting upset or hostile during an interview.

6   Approaching Studios

A quick and easy way to monitor job opportunities is using RSS feeds.[15] RSS feeds are similar to news headlines for a particular website. Feeds update automatically. When you log into your feed reader, you see the newest job postings. You don't need to thumb through multiple webpages to find the same information.

RSS feeds also help you track industry trends. When you see one particular position posted at a studio—cinematic artist, for example—other studios start posting for the same discipline. There are usually sporadic periods when studios list multiple job openings for the same position, followed by a drought for that discipline.

Game studios seem to procrastinate job postings until they absolutely need employees. Then, they post many jobs in one fell swoop. An opportunity may come and go in just a few weeks. Timing is everything; if you already submitted your application, you improve your chances when you submit another. You want your application to be fresh in the lists, right when studios are poised to hire.

In school, apply for jobs four to six weeks *before* you graduate. This gives studios time to respond, and it gives you a chance to line something up before graduation. You must commit yourself to finishing your projects before the end of the term to include them in your portfolio. A few weeks of nonstop work to avoid months of unemployment are well worth it!

The easiest time to get hired is straight out of college, because employers are eager for new talent. If you miss that window and a few months pass after you graduate, studios begin to question secretly why you haven't found a job. The application process becomes more stressful and takes longer.

---

15. RSS, or really simple syndication, is a standardized publication format. Homepages, like google.com/ig or netvibes.com, include RSS feed readers.

Opportunities don't come to you; you must seek them out to create the ideal situation. There's no "perfect time," so it's a waste of opportunity to wait. Entice studios to talk with you by contacting them first. When you get their attention, your portfolio convinces studios that you are the right candidate to hire.

7 Working with Recruiters and Headhunters

Recruiters and headhunters charge fees, but they provide access to many different studios, when they're well connected. Recruiters and headhunters ask about your interests and skills in attempt to find the right match for you. They use your resume and references to pair you with a studio. Think of recruiters and headhunters as middlemen who position your portfolio in front of a studio.

8   Keeping Perspective

When you hate the world, the world hates you back. Likewise, when you love the world, the world loves you back. There is a saying that, "You attract more flies with honey than vinegar."

It's important to apply this mentality when you attend game developer conferences, speak with industry professionals, and interview with studios. Don't assume that attendees don't want you there simply because the game industry is difficult to get into. Don't think that you are entitled to a job, either, but studios "refuse" to give you a chance. This mentality builds to eventually explode as negative confrontations that look bad on your record. Instead, keep an open mind, and ask polite questions. Convince people that it's hard *not* to hire you, because you are so darn likeable.

An office manager who screened application emails before they reached HR remarked about the brashness of one student's email. The student wrote that his portfolio was "so good it makes your eyes bleed!"

This arrogant move sent the message that the student was too good for that studio. In reality, studios need you just as much as you need them. That doesn't mean they can't find someone else in a heartbeat—especially for entry-level positions—so avoid blemishes on your rapport. That office manager unashamedly said that she blacklisted that student who made the arrogant email comment.

This is just an example of how the words you choose reflect your personality. Show your enthusiasm and professionalism in phone conversations, emails, and other forms of communication.

Interactions between applicants and HR employees usually occur digitally, through email. Double-check your spelling and grammar, and use stimulating words with exclamation points, where appropriate.

9   Applying for Positions Requiring More Experience

People often apply to lower-level jobs because they feel unqualified for higher-paying jobs. A story on National Public Radio revealed that a significantly smaller number of applicants applied for a position with higher pay, even when applicants qualified for the higher-paying job.[16] Applicants reason that lower-paying jobs are easier to get because the jobs paid less. Applicants thought they gave employers a break, because they were overqualified for the lower-paying position. Employees are willing to sacrifice for a better chance to be hired.

In reality, lower-paying jobs are more competitive, because everyone thinks the same thing. You should not limit yourself by thinking that you aren't qualified. Studios want employees with good track records, and sometimes they create new positions, tailored to candidates' skill levels, instead of waiting for adept candidates.

When you have the skill, but you lack the experience on paper, apply anyway. The worst a screener can do is to deny your application, and everybody moves on. Screeners might alert you about new positions matching your qualifications.

---

16. Noguchi, Yuki. "Help Wanted. But Not For Mid-Level Jobs." National Public Radio: 2012.

10   Fending Off Competition

The more fun a job appears, the more competition exists between applicants. For example, traditional artists such as painters and illustrators struggle to develop sustainable careers. They dream of selling art at galleries and earning their livings with their own unique ideas and styles. Little demand exists for this type of art.

In school, most illustration majors targeted video games in order to earn a living. Illustrators live and breathe traditional painting, and they devise new ideas at the snap of a finger. Illustrators find concept jobs before the students who pursue broad game-development majors.

The same goes for programming. Computer science majors write code incessantly, and they have the best programming skills. Generic game development majors target *game design*. If you're an artist or programmer, earn a specialized degree to gain a competitive advantage. While earning your degree, befriend game development students, and join their mod teams.

With the increasing reality of outsourcing, thriving as a traditional artist is becoming more difficult in the video game industry. Your success depends on networking and making a name for yourself. A general rule of thumb is that the more technical and less appealing a task (e.g. programming, rigging, technical art), the less competition, and the less important networking becomes when you're finding a job. Those technical jobs require talent, alone.

11   Approaching Studios Professionally

A woman in a car in the parking lot at a studio asked a group of developers whether she needed a degree to qualify for a job at the company. The employees ignored her, until one man finally replied, politely, that she should direct her questions to HR or refer to the company's website. Hers was not the best of strategies. She was unprofessional, and people did not want to help her, because they did not know her or her intentions.

Instead of appearing at a company's door, reach out to other studio employees, indirectly, through forums, friends of friends, conferences, and group lunches.

One man dressed in a storm trooper costume and entered the Epic Games building without an appointment. He got a job, but only because the president *already knew about his work*. His portfolio must have been exceptional for the president to know about it. If his portfolio stank, and he pulled a stunt like that, he wouldn't have had a thread of a chance. His costume would have been an entertaining moment for employees, and nothing more. He was the right *person* in front of the right people.

12   Uncovering the Hidden Job Market

Studies prove that 80% of all jobs are unadvertised,[17] and only 5% of job seekers obtain jobs through ads.[18] Only 5%! This statistic is especially true in the video game industry. Most advertised job openings get hundreds, and even thousands, of applicants. Thus, to shorten the process and avoid filtering through the applicants, studios usually search for candidates without advertising positions to the public.

A hiring agency randomly contacted me about a new *Halo* title. At first, I thought the agency was fraudulent. When I realized that it was legitimate, my experience proved the notion that most jobs lack official help-wanted postings. Studios prefer to operate under the radar.

Check igda.org, the website for the International Game Developers Association, IGDA. Its jobs section advertises local jobs with less competition than the big, national, listings. Join your local IGDA chapter. Local studios post job openings on the chapter forums. You can set up email alerts to receive notifications.

You can find other useful groups on LinkedIn.com. Set up your account to receive email updates from group discussions and job postings. Popular LinkedIn.com game development groups include Unreal Developers Group, IGDA, Android Developers Group, Game Developers, and Women in Games International. You can also check a few game industry HR managers' LinkedIn.com profiles, because they are often members of popular game development groups.

Another place to find job listings is craigslist.org. Many applicants discount craigslist.org as second best, assuming it lacks substantial listings. Because applicants don't look there,

---

17. Dickler, Jessica. "The hidden job market," *CNN Money,* June 10, 2009, http://money.cnn.com/2009/06/09/news/economy/hidden_jobs.
18. Hansen, Randall S. Ph.D. *Quintessential Careers;* "15 Myths and Misconceptions About Job-Hunting."

fewer qualified candidates apply. That gives you a better chance at those positions. People keep job postings available on craigslist.org for a short time. When you see an applicable job posting, apply promptly.

You can learn about unpublished job openings when you attend meetings of your local video game developer chapter, such as IGDA. Befriend other developers in your area. They might be turned off if you ask about jobs upfront, so engage in a casual conversation. When it's appropriate, subtly inquire about open positions.

III. GETTING HIRED

1   Getting Your Foot in the Door

When you're established in the industry, you might receive unexpected calls from other studios. They might ask if you're interested in a job. This is a *great* problem to have! Most jobs are unadvertised or limited to referral candidates. When studios exhaust those candidates, they seek the best-known industry professionals. Studios typically offer temporary positions to younger professionals, because younger people are usually more willing to accept them.

Advertise your name among industry websites and magazines. Start a popular thread on a forum. Become well known on forums like polycount.com, forums.epicgames.com, CGHub.com, ConceptArt.org, ZBrushCentral.com, and NeoGAF.com. Studios should encounter your name frequently when they search for new candidates online.

I submitted an environment scene that was featured in the exhibition section of a major digital art magazine. If you are an artist, submit artwork to a 3D Art magazine. If you're a designer, get your mod or game recognized within a community, and win competitions.

Now that the *Unreal Editor*, now called the *Unreal Developer's Kit*, is mainstream, competitions using the engine are more difficult and require bigger teams. Epic and Intel host an annual contest, called Make Something Unreal (www.MakeSomethingUnreal.com). The entries improve every year, and entering the contest helps you test your skills and determine what others are doing. For artists, top contests include Dominance War (DominanceWar.com), Unearthly Challenge (UnearthlyChallenge.com), and the Polycount Competitions (polycount.com).

Well-known competitions for design and programming include the annual Indie Game Challenge (IndieGameChallenge.com), which showcases the best qualifiers at GDC. Qualifiers also receive hefty scholarships. Also, Global

Game Jam (GlobalGameJam.org) is a competition with a theme provided, and entrants must craft an entire game prototype in forty-eight hours. This helps you quickly gain credibility, because you compete globally. The competition is short, so it doesn't prevent you from enjoying life. Global Game Jam posts webcams online, so you observe global competitors. If you attend a good game development school, and you intend to focus on design, you should participate in this competition. Some programs include competitions as class projects, a great way to kill two birds with one stone!

Overall, competitions are less stressful than mods, because they involve smaller teams or solo work. Competitions have deadlines, so it's realistic to expect the world to see your product before a slower mod fizzles out. Competitions also provide quick motivation, and you can list them on your resume. Cliff Bleszinski, creative director of Epic Games, landed his first job at Epic by entering design competitions.

Keep in mind, your competitors are industry professionals strutting their talent and proving themselves to the world. They have more skill than students. Students and aspiring developers have an advantage in these competitions, though, because many developers consider themselves too busy to dedicate adequate time to competitions.

Choose a studio, and tailor your design to the studio's style. Blizzard Entertainment produces stylized fantasy role-playing games every year. Blizzard looks for candidates who can produce its style, and *only* its style. You might get frustrated if you're interested in two different studios with conflicting styles or design principles. Smaller studios *do* prefer versatility to produce a variety of games, though, so it's in your favor to vary your portfolio (in case you have trouble getting hired by a studio with your similar style).

You might also target a genre of game instead of an actual studio. For example, a warzone environment is compatible to many game studios producing first-person shooters. Sadly, many studios base games on war and shooting. Use this to your advantage to appeal to a broad range of studios.

I maintain a spreadsheet listing the companies that interest me, organized by priority. In the document, I've added links to studios' websites and information about their hiring status. You can create a similar cheat sheet about your options, analyze your goals, and figure out where you want to work. After you create a list, it's easier to determine which studio to target.

How do you know whether a studio is *the right one*? After you've done a variety of previous game development, you probably know which style you prefer. The style you prefer is probably the same style as the games you play. Be careful with this strategy, because when you work on the type of games you love, you might enjoy playing them less.

A senior-level artist on a stylized game told me that he chooses studios that produce the type of art that he created in his spare time. This way, he doesn't go home after his workdays and spend extra hours developing games for fulfillment.

Other professionals agree with this concept, suggesting that when you contribute to projects you disagree with, it is therapeutic to work at home on personal projects that you enjoy.

A business team member (non-developer) told me that every studio where he applied indicated that he didn't have enough experience, but he was a good cultural fit. He suggested that in the game industry, as long as he faked the cultural fit, then he was in. For example, when he said his favorite game was *Psychonauts*, or that he loved the art style in *Okami*, his interviewers drooled.

The colleague said that games must be critically acclaimed but not good sellers, because developers love the technically superb games that are misunderstood by the public. This is the attitude of a true insider. I don't recommend faking cultural fit, especially if you are not already gamer by nature. Otherwise, people quickly realize that you are less interested in video games than you originally claimed to be.

2   Outsourcing

Working for an outsourcer can get your foot in the door when you're new to the field, but it should be your last resort. My friend from school lives in China working for Ubisoft Entertainment S.A. . She claims she has opportunities to move up quickly in China, but she misses home. I assume the pay is lower and the hours are merciless working in outsourcing studios—especially in China. Working for an outsourcing studio might be a great way to improve your skills, but it might also hinder your career when you return to your native country and seek a new job.

3   Being Persistent

Persistence is the key to getting what you want in life. A college friend had trouble finding a job, so I helped him develop his skills. But I still felt his skills were inadequate for a major studio. One year after graduation, he attended GDC, and he landed a job at a social games studio in San Francisco. Not too shabby!

Finding a job takes constant persistence. You must stay in front of the studios with the budgets and desire to hire additional employees. My friend might have found a job faster if he'd applied a better work ethic in school. He also lived with his parents after he graduated, and his parents paid for his trips to these conferences. Every situation is different, and not everyone can attend conferences. So, be patient; your talent and connections with developers give you the edge to find a job.

4   Knowing People Doesn't Guarantee You a Job

A seasoned artist was obsessed with Blizzard Entertainment . He had friends who boasted about their roles at Blizzard. They told him about the skillful management and delightful pay. Through his connections at the studio, he landed multiple art tests and interviews.

He attempted not one, but *four* art tests, throughout the span of two years. After each test, the studio declined to hire him, because his skills didn't meet expectations. Reportedly, Blizzard requires applicants to wait six months between art tests.

This battle-hardened artist spent years improving his skills to submit improved art tests. Every year, the studio expected more. Despite his efforts to improve, he still hasn't met the studio's expectations. His problem was not working *hard enough* on his portfolio. He would always talk about working on his portfolio, but in reality, he was probably playing online games at home. His shy and forgettable personality is another barrier between him and his success.

Blizzard Entertainment archives previous art tests, and hiring managers compare applicants' progress between their old and new tests. Keep trying; be persistent without giving up— especially for your dream studio.

5   Taking the QA Route

When all else fails, try quality assurance. Testing is the lowest position in the game industry. It requires the least amount of experience, and jobs are the most volatile. Studios producing single-player games with teams of ten to twenty testers eliminate the entire team or reduce the team to a single tester by the end of production.

Studios often separate QA from the rest of the team to prevent testers from influencing the actual game production. Don't expect to enter the industry in QA and add new ideas to games. Adding new ideas is a designer's job. The sole purpose of QA testers is finding bugs in games and reporting the bugs to multiple departments.

QA is usually the last position filled on a project, and it's the first to get cut. If you want to be a tester, stay current. During interviews for QA positions, expect interviewers to ask which games you play, which games are your favorites, and why. Prepare to demonstrate a short playtest on an actual game. This exercise demonstrates your ability to think critically about games. Show them that you can play games to *find errors*—not just for fun.

With these simple tips, you can get a job in QA, without previous experience in the game industry. Follow these tips for QA playtests:

- Walk along the corners of rooms, where holes in the collision are most prevalent.
- Jump down into death pits to verify that characters respawn properly.
- Playing with the controller behind your back, with opposite hands, or with your eyes closed are ways to find new issues that you had not considered.

You learn most QA skills on the job. Testers should get creative, because testing gets *really* repetitive, *really* fast.

6   Getting Out of QA

Most people don't want to stay in QA forever. The best way escape QA is to become a top performer in your department. QA is all about numbers, and studios track testing by bugs opened and closed each day. When you enter the most bugs, and you're known for your familiarity with the game, influential studio leaders notice you.

Studios expect testers on single-player games to enter at least twelve bugs daily, and fifteen bugs on average. Top-performing testers enter up to forty bugs daily. Testers moving into design roles are among these top performers. Bug numbers alone don't get you out of QA; bug numbers just earn recognition from the QA lead. But, QA leads don't make hiring decisions for other departments.

To earn a promotion from QA, develop additional skills. Many testers learn about design, because design is closely related to testing. When you're a game tester, open the studio's game editor, and create practice levels. If the game engine is not installed on your system, ask a designer, your lead, or the IT department to install it for you.

When you create a practice level, ask designers for feedback. Show them how quickly you implement the changes they recommend. This proven strategy might help you become one of many designers who start in QA. Design departments look for creative testers to join their teams.

Moving from QA to design is harder in big studios, where QA departments are often *completely* separated from development teams. Bigger studios often restrict testers' access to game editors.

You should research the QA department before you sign on with a studio when you intend to try for a design position. Observe whether interviewers mention previous testers moving into developer positions. If the studio offers a tour, determine whether QA is situated near the design team.

When you identify a studio that encourages growth from testing to other disciplines, and you develop your skills, QA is an excellent way into the industry.

Be humble. Many developers consider QA teams beneath them. Therefore, they expect QA employees to be courteous and polite, because testers haven't earned their say yet. Cocky QA employees get fired for back-talking developers or publically calling their designs stupid. Developers might not receive equal punishment, because they are harder to replace.

7   Working on a Mod

Creating a *mod* means modifying an existing game using the same engine for an entirely new gaming experience. Fans often create mods to share ideas with other game fans. Within the last few years, mods became a competitive way to rally a team and compile short, professional quality gameplay experiences.

Studios often expect that students and aspiring developers complete mod projects to demonstrate scheduling and provide examples of in-game functionality. What type of mod should you do? How do you know whether a mod is right for you? Are mods *really* important?

Because mods are increasingly professional, successful mods are also organized. Mod leaders should define milestones and separate tasks for team members to track the mod's progress.

When you contribute to a mod, *attend milestone meetings.* If mod leaders don't set project milestones, they aren't serious about the project. If you are a member of a mod with team members uncommitted to the project, suggest enforcing project milestones.

I participated on a mod team that conducted biweekly milestone meetings over *Skype,* the popular video and text chat application. We used text chat, exclusively. The meetings help communicate what team members were doing and planned to do next, similar to the "scrum" system of professional development in the game industry.

At GDC 2009 in San Francisco, a programmer at Valve Software said that Valve mainly hires applicants from the mod community. When you work on a successful mod and gain a loyal following, *only then* does Valve show interest in you. Their strategy is similar to booking the Super Bowl halftime show; the organizers consider only the most popular performers, because those performers draw huge audiences. The performers' previous success and popularity bring more success.

A colleague told me about a full-time mod project that went nowhere, because team members' commitments varied. He said to ensure that all mod team members are equally dedicated to finishing the project and going public with the mod. Otherwise, the project might falter. People often start mods with online-only contacts, people they haven't met in person. It's difficult to analyze a stranger's level of contribution or trust. Team members are initially excited about the mod, but many drop out a few weeks later.

I've had similar experiences. I received an email invitation to join an existing mod. The mod seemed promising, and the mod leader had his act together. About half of the team members were industry professionals, which reassured me. However, team members dropped out when tasks weren't completed on schedule. Team members stopped attending meetings. The college students quit first, because they were engaged in multiple mods. They quickly diverted their attention to other, more successful mods. Some college students accepted job offers and abandoned the mod.

Although some industry professionals stayed with the mod, they weren't committed. The most talented member quit because the deadlines were too strict. He told me in a personal email that he quit because he wanted to have a life. He valued his friends, and he wanted to have fun during his free time.

I didn't enjoy facing tight deadlines at my day job and coming home to *yet another tight deadline!* Mod deadlines are especially frustrating when you aren't convinced about the mod's chances for success, or if you are the only one pulling most of the weight. Mods are hard work, and they're even harder for professionals who already work overtime and barely have enough time for their lives.

I left the mod after I completed the art for one level. I wanted to focus on buying a house at the time, and I was juggling too many obligations.

An art director for Disney said that you should focus on one task at a time, in three-month intervals, to get things done.

You can do a lot in three months. When you dedicate yourself to something whole-heartedly, your efforts provide fruitful rewards. When you finish a project, you can invest the same focus to the next one. Each project is stronger, because it receives your full attention. Your personal life thanks you, too.

8   Signing Noncompete Clauses

Some studios include noncompete clauses in employee contracts, limiting employees from publishing games they design outside office hours—even at home—especially when the style resembles the studio's games. Enforcement of noncompete clauses seems lenient. Veterans reveal stories about keeping freelance projects under the table and making sure projects don't interfere with their work. Studio managers prefer that you don't tell them about your ideas or personal projects. They'd rather claim ignorance when you get sued.

In short, noncompete clauses should not scare you away from your hobby. Studios expect you to practice during your own time to progress your talent.

One colleague, weary that he might not legally own his personal video game-related work based on the noncompete clause, decided to pursue photography and film in his spare time instead of video games. Because photography and film are so different from video games, these projects couldn't compete with video games, and he didn't violate his noncompete clause.

A group of programmers left a comfortable AAA studio because they didn't want to risk losing ownership of an idea. These programmers were passionate about creating a smartphone game, and they found day jobs programming for an unrelated industry while they developed the smartphone game. The group's leader assumed that software industries outside games might be more flexible with copyright laws. When you're not sure whether your projects outside the office are restricted by your contract, you should consult an expert for advice.

9   Practicing Your Elevator Speech

Your elevator speech summarizes your experience and accomplishments as efficiently and clearly as possible, within ten minutes. Use body language and analogies to complement your story. The imagery helps people without industry knowledge to understand you. Describe your skills, and explain why you enjoy your work. Every time you rehearse your elevator speech at parties or with friends, it becomes more refined.

Is it insincere to memorize your speech and your responses to typically asked questions? No! In fact, it's more appealing when you flow your words together. Memorization keeps your speech concise, so you don't babble. A rehearsed elevator speech also shows forethought and planning. You are good at developing video games. Now, demonstrate your understanding of your field by artfully articulating your job description.

When you attend enough networking events, you will eventually meet one of your idols—someone you've always wanted to work for. But, you have his or her attention only for a few minutes. Don't miss the chance to communicate your suitability to work with your idol. Tasteful self-promotion is expected during interviews and at networking parties. Your elevator speech must sound enthusiastically genuine, and you should focus objectively on your strengths, instead of senselessly bragging or putting other people down.

10   Interviewing

Job interviews are daunting and intimidating. For most candidates, interviews make the difference between getting a job and walking home empty handed. Arrive prepared. Get in the right mindset, and your interviewer senses your enthusiasm and confidence.

All interviews are different, but interviewers use common practices, industry-wide. Expect the following events in a typical interview process:

1. **Phone screenings:** For out-of-state and higher-level positions, studios usually conduct phone screenings before in-house interviews. Sometimes studios bypass phone screenings for entry-level and local candidates. Unsuitable applicants with recommendations usually receive polite rejection emails. Unsuitable applicants without referrals usually don't receive responses.

2. **In-house interviews:** You meet face-to-face with a leader at the studio. An invitation to an in-house interview shows the studio's interest in you, and it allows the studio to determine whether you're interesting, whether you can hold a conversation, and whether you'd fit into the studio's culture. Studios sometimes conduct these interviews virtually using *Skype* or other teleconferencing software to save money.

3. **Hiring decision:** After reviewing potential candidates for a position, the studio makes a decision. The studio contacts you with a job offer or rejection email, depending on the decision.

LinkedIn.com is an essential online networking tool for job seekers. It might surprise you, though, to know that LinkedIn.com can also help you ace the interview. Before an interview, request the names of your interviewers. Do your homework. Use LinkedIn.com to research your interviewers' backgrounds. Check out your interviewers' experience, philosophies, and interests. When they don't post much information on their LinkedIn.com profiles, use a search engine to look for personal websites, or search on social networking sites such as Facebook to find information.

It's a small world, and you share more in common with your interviewers than you might expect. People naturally enjoy talking about themselves, so when you subtly reveal a shared interest, they feel more connected to you.

I knew a friend of my interviewer at one studio, but I didn't find this out until I asked about the interviewer's past at EA Sports. After we established the common relationship, the conversation took off, and we discussed various topics. The more we bonded, the more he wanted to hire me.

Don't be disappointed when your interview conversation seems stale or unexciting. Studios emphasize that interviewers should remain politically correct to avoid perception of impropriety that might lead to a lawsuit. Studios might lose more money from one discriminating interview than they lose by hiring a dozen mediocre employees. It's safe to assume, however, that when the interview conversation starts great but fades, you're not making a good impression. To mitigate the damage, be proactive and control the mood of the interview. Make the interview as fun and interesting as possible. Match your interviewer's energy. But when he or she is just plain boring, just be you. You shouldn't be forced to be boring, too.

11   Answering Typical Interview Questions

Before your interview, research websites for examples of typical interview questions. You can expect to answer the following questions during a game industry interview:

- What games do you play?
- Which game is your favorite, and why?
- Do you know how to use _____ program?
  Determine which software the studio uses beforehand, and make sure you know it—at least moderately. If you are unfamiliar with the software, use your time before the interview to practice with a trial version.
- Name a time you went beyond the call of duty on a certain task.
  An example could be that you noticed a problem in another department's workflow, so you politely suggested a new strategy to the lead of that department. Keep a list of your successes and best moments throughout the years.
- Do you know about our company and how it was founded?
  Check Wikipedia.org or the company's website before your interview.
- What would you change about your last studio?
  Be careful here: Don't make negative or opinionated remarks about previous employers. Be objective, and restrict your response to only one opportunity for improvement. Never discuss faults related to a particular person. Share a creative idea, such as putting the QA team closer to developers, scheduling lunches for developers in cross-disciplines to get to know each other, or adding instructional classes given by the seniors at the studio.
- What are your greatest strength and weakness in the game industry?
  During an impromptu interview at GDC during a party, the interviewer told me that he expected my response to

the weaknesses question to be "None." He seemed ego-driven, and others might actually be repelled by this response. A good manager realizes that nobody is perfect.

A Sample Interview

The following sample interview uses fictitious names and paraphrases an actual interview for a QA position. CANDIDATE is applying for a job, SHIRLEY is the HR representative, and BLAKE is the producer.

SHIRLEY greets CANDIDATE at the studio when CANDIDATE arrives for the interview.

SHIRLEY   The salary expectations you listed on your application are out of our range. Are you flexible about compensation?

CANDIDATE   Yes.

SHIRLEY   Okay, I wanted to make sure you were flexible before we begin.

SHIRLEY writes "flexible" in the paperwork's salary section.

SHIRLEY   Do you have any questions?

CANDIDATE   Not at the moment, thank you.

SHIRLEY   Okay, Blake will be in shortly.

CANDIDATE picks up a video game magazine from a desk nearby to show her interest in the studio's game.
Knock on door.

SHIRLEY   Hi, Candidate, here's Blake.

BLAKE   First off, do you know about our company and how it started?

It's a good thing that CANDIDATE did her research. She didn't find much information about the studio online, but she made the most of what she found by reciting the general information that she read online, which was better than nothing.

BLAKE I see that you worked for Superlative Games. Describe your experience. What would you change about the way things were done?

CANDIDATE Stress levels were high because of crunch, and everyone talked about how many hours they worked. But, people handled it pretty well without letting it affect their work. If management organized for crunch better, employees would be more willing to work there.

CANDIDATE made sure not to be too negative or point out anyone specific.

BLAKE What are your strengths and weaknesses in the game industry?

CANDIDATE My attention to detail is my greatest strength. I like to add fine detail to everything I touch. Making something great the first time takes a little more time, but it's worth it in the end. And I don't have to go back to fix it later.

As for my biggest weakness, well, weaknesses are always hard! I would say my weakness is that I don't always know when to call my work done. Sometimes I keep tweaking it. I reach a point when players don't notice the difference. I am learning to draw the line and stop when I achieve the appropriate level of detail.

CANDIDATE threw in a recovery for her weakness to make it a strength.

BLAKE Do you have any questions?

CANDIDATE   I am interested in your role in production. Do you deal with the media and marketing? I checked out your LinkedIn.com profile, and I read that you were previously a programmer. Do you miss programming?

BLAKE, intrigued, said that he misses programming sometimes, but he finds production just as fulfilling. He programs at home to fill the void.

BLAKE   Candidate, I see you pursued an artist position recently. Is that where you want to end up in video games?

Candidate   Yes.

BLAKE   Do you know anything about *Maya*?

CANDIDATE   I'm good in *Maya*, and I'm excellent in *3DS Max*. I go back and forth between them. I had access to the files in my last job. When I found art bugs, I just went in quickly and fixed them. When I couldn't fix something, I suggested the fix to the QA team. They were busy, so I usually input the bugs, myself.

BLAKE   Thanks for your time, Candidate. Nice to meet you! You meet Harry and Vincent next.

Enter HARRY (producer) and VINCENT (QA lead).

VINCENT   Tell me about your bug implementation process. What did you include in bug descriptions?

CANDIDATE   I always included a screenshot, because that helped the artists. I included the level name and what I was doing to produce the bug. We didn't have saved games, so I pointed out how to get to the area quickest or indicated the file name.

VINCENT   Was there a time you had a bug that you felt was important, but it came back from the developer as a check-failed, meaning the developer would review it later, if ever?

CANDIDATE   When I felt strongly about the bug, I talked with that developer directly, listing my reasons why it was important to fix the bug. When the developer still thought fixing the bug wasn't worthwhile, there wasn't much I could do. I let the developer make the final decision.

HARRY   Tell me more about the art contracting you did while you were in college.

CANDIDATE   I had an unpaid internship arranged by the school. We created artwork based on the studio's guidelines, and the producer and environment artist checked the progress of our work. They provided screenshots, with tips about improving the art. At the end of the course, they conducted a conference call with the class. I had a whole list of questions to ask, because I was curious about the industry.

HARRY   I saw that you worked on a plane-flying simulation. That sounds pretty cool. Could you tell me more about it?

CANDIDATE   Yes. The project was requested by a history museum with a generic shooting game that really wasn't much. They wanted a better playing experience. They had the shell of a real-life bomber plane's cockpit, and they wanted the audience to step inside and use a screen to simulate dropping a bomb.

I was doing programming and art, and I was about to graduate. I didn't have time to contribute to the project. The person representing the museum left before I graduated. I'm not sure whether the project was ever finished.

HARRY   Could you describe what you did at Superlative Games and what you learned?

CANDIDATE   I learned about setting up breakables and modeling collision, and I helped with various tasks for the team. I also made suggestions and volunteered to complete different tasks.

VINCENT   Tell us about a time you went beyond the call of duty on a certain task.

CANDIDATE   I have many examples. When I edited files and discovered problems, I fixed the problems and often discovered additional problems in the process. I fixed those problems, too, instead of entering more bugs and taking extra time to have them assigned back to me.

In another instance, I took a destroyed van and impaled it with a spike in a lava valley.

CANDIDATE uses hand gestures to describe the process.

My lead thought the van was cool, showed the art director, and they kept it in the game. They liked my improvisation.

Another time, I suggested changing cars at the bottom of a canyon. They had supposedly fallen off high cliffs, but the cars looked too neatly placed—like a parking lot.

At first, I don't think the artist considered it. But, after my suggestion, he starting flipping the cars and used more freedom placing the cars, like placing them on their backs and sides. We had the texture artist update the bottoms of the vehicles, because the bottom used a low-res texture. I believe rearranging those cars added more believability to the game.

VINCENT   Give me an example of how you'd find and input a bug.

CANDIDATE   I usually went along walls and jumped up and down, trying to hit a stair step and get caught in the collision. Then, I tried to fight enemies in different ways, instead of going straight at them.

VINCENT   What bug were you most proud about finding?

CANDIDATE   I found a bug by jumping along the side of a mountain range, and I got on top and behind the geometry. I got stuck on the other side. That was a game blocker, and I'm glad I found it because it might have been overlooked.

HARRY   Do you have any questions for us?

CANDIDATE   *Directed to VINCENT:* What's the funniest bug you've come across?

VINCENT   Wow, she put me on the spot!

VINCENT answers about a character stealing items from non-player characters without the non-player characters acknowledging it.

HARRY   How do you feel about crunching? Are you comfortable with it?

CANDIDATE   Yes, sadly, I'm actually accustomed to crunch. I enjoy the challenge. Do you have to crunch weekends frequently?

HARRY   We try to keep weekends free. It's important to us, here. Also, we only expect the department that's behind to crunch—not the entire studio.

CANDIDATE   *Directed to HARRY:* Do you think creating a more innocent game adds to a happier company culture than doing death research for sinister games?

HARRY   I wouldn't say it keeps stress levels down, but it's cool to see everyone on YouTube watching cartoons for research instead of tweaking a bone pile for hours.

HARRY   We'll bring in a game for the *PS3* and get you to play it. I'll get Blake.

HARRY leaves and returns.

HARRY   Blake was busy, but we can do this, anyway.

HARRY starts a dinosaur game. Although CANDIDATE had a bad impression of the game and read negative online reviews about it, she didn't share her opinion.

Keeping her opinions to herself paid off. The game was developed by another studio closely related to the company. The interviewers would not appreciate negative comments.

HARRY   This game is the product of our sister company. Describe what you're doing and your decisions while you're playing.

CANDIDATE plays the game, jumping around walls and into a death pit to verify that the character dies. CANDIDATE shoots dinosaurs after they're dead to ensure nothing funny or unexpected happens.

HARRY   Do you have any other questions?

CANDIDATE Based on my interview today, are there any obstacles preventing you from offering me this position?

CANDIDATE rehearsed this question. She read it on a popular job advice website, and she thought that it was a provocative and interesting question to spice up the interview.

HARRY   Wow, that's a good question! I can't really think of anything. You present yourself well, and you're a gamer. You just haven't had a chance to do actual QA before.

VINCENT   Are you sure you would consider a QA position that isn't art-related? You have other ways to get into the game industry. Some people don't consider QA. We've already had two designers move up from QA here at the studio!

VINCENT subtly mentioned the opportunities at this studio beyond QA.

CANDIDATE Yes, I understand that this position involves QA, and I'm fine with that.

HARRY   I don't have any more questions. Thanks for your time.

VINCENT and HARRY leave. SHIRLEY returns.

SHIRLEY   Well, CANDIDATE, do you have any remaining questions?

CANDIDATE   No, thank you. Everyone was helpful.

SHIRLEY   I will give you a studio tour now.

CANDIDATE   Awesome!

CANDIDATE shows enthusiasm at every opportunity.

CANDIDATE   Will you contact me to tell me whether I've got the job?

SHIRLEY   Yes, we will contact you by next Wednesday to let you know, either way.

CANDIDATE closely observes SHIRLEY'S body language and her choice of words to gauge the likelihood of a job offer.

CANDIDATE wanted to thank the interviewers. SHIRLEY didn't provide the interviewers' email addresses, so CANDIDATE proactively added the interviewers as contacts on LinkedIn.com and included thank-you notes with her contact requests.

12   Saving Salary Discussions for HR

Don't ask about salaries until you reach the end of the interview. Even then, you can wait. HR representatives might ask about your desired salary during phone screenings, cutting you off at the knees before you have a chance to negotiate.

Industry veterans might circumvent this question better than newcomers. When interviewers ask you about salary early on, suggest a $15,000 range within your comfort level. Do your research, and your expected salary should be in the middle of that range, or possibly near the lower end. For example, when you know that the position pays around $40,000 per year, request a salary ranging from $35,000–$50,000. This gives the studio an opportunity to woo you with an offer over $40,000. It also shows your flexibility, because you set your minimum under the average. Most studios don't offer the minimum salary from your desired salary range, because it sends the message that the studio doesn't value your opinion. You should research salary reports to set reasonable expectations.

Heed the advice from HR managers, who encourage salary discussions with HR managers—not interviewers.[19] When you interview with employees outside HR, they probably don't influence your salary. Other studio employees typically direct you to HR for salary discussions. You also don't want your interviewers to think you're pushing respect barriers. Interviewers want to learn about you, so they can decide whether your skills and personality are a good fit. Interviewers might not have authority, nor do they want the responsibility, of salary decisions.

---

19. Walker, Deborah. "Avoid These 10 Job Interview Bloopers—Critical Job-Seeker Mistakes," accessed July 4, 2012, http://www.quintcareers.com/interview_mistakes.html.

13   Conducting Informational Interviews

An informational interview allows you to ask studio employees about a company's working conditions and processes. Ask someone at a convention, "May I please have fifteen minutes of your time to gather your opinions about your studio?"

Do not indicate that you're looking for a job, and remember to thank your interviewee for his or her time. Restrict the duration of the interview to the agreed-upon amount of time.

Ask, "What skills and traits do you seek for candidates in the _____ discipline?"

Studios are organized differently. A programmer from Valve Software explained that Valve divides each team into smaller teams, called *cabals*, including an employee from each discipline. A studio might have structures or policies that bother you, and it is better to learn sooner rather than later.

When your interviewee works in a different discipline, he or she offers valuable information about your discipline from experiences with colleagues. In fact, you might learn *facts that are more interesting* about your discipline from someone who isn't in it.

Numerous college professors and industry speakers advise candidates to water down technical industry jargon during conversations with HR representatives. HR representatives might be unfamiliar with precise terms. However, HR representatives, from my experience, use as much jargon as everyone else—although they might not know exactly what the words mean. Candidates might include game-industry lingo to demonstrate industry awareness, without going overboard.

14   Contracting and Third-Party Staffing Agencies

When you find a job as a contract employee, which is growing more common, a staffing agency employs you. You file new-hire paperwork proving your qualifications to work for the studio, and the staffing agency asks you a few questions. The staffing agency might arrange direct deposit. Afterward, you rarely interact with the agency, unless there is a problem with your hours or you need to update your account. You work for the studio, and the staffing agency serves as a third party, similar to your banker.

One disadvantage of employment through a contract agency is that you receive fewer benefits than studio employees. Also, contract employees typically don't qualify for discounts or promotions available to regular employees. When the studio hires you full-time, you complete a huge pile of additional paperwork to transfer your title. At that point, you may apply for improved benefits, such as a 401(k) retirement plan.

15   Dressing for the Industry

"If you come to an interview at Epic wearing a suit and tie, we will cut off the tie and hang it on our wall of shame."

—Michael Capps, President, Epic Games

Dressing appropriately in the game industry is more like solving a Rubik's cube than a crossword puzzle. The industry shares little documentation about dress expectations for interviews, and it's important to get it right. When you stray too far from your interviewers' style, they suspect that you don't conform to the company's culture. Dress your "Sunday best," but don't go overboard. Don't outdo your potential boss in terms of dress.

Ask the interview coordinator about dress code before an interview. Generally, I recommend collared shirts with nice jeans for men, and comfortable dresses or blouses with dress jeans for women.

As an intern, I tried to impress coworkers by wearing chinos during my first weeks on the job. I came from the retail industry, which has a more traditional business-casual dress code. My chinos didn't make the impression I'd intended. The creative director and design director wore jeans and t-shirts, and colleagues assumed I didn't get the culture.

As Mike Capps of Epic Games explained, you shouldn't wear a suit and tie to an interview. Capps' interviewee awkwardly noticed that studio employees wore informal clothes, and he progressively loosened his tie, unbuttoned his collar, and removed his coat throughout his interview.

The interviewee said, "Wow, your studio is much less serious than I expected."

Altogether, this did not go over well. The interviewee did not anticipate his audience, and he insulted the studio. He did not get the job.

16   Harvesting Confidence

Like it or not, America, and many other areas, are increasingly "loud" societies. With people making quick decisions among distractions, artificial confidence is just as convincing as real confidence. Confidence is a state of mind. Convince yourself that you are special, and you express your ability to do well.

Problems occur when people appear overconfident and don't live up to their hype. These people make it harder to separate the wheat from the chaff when studios make hiring decisions. When you fake confidence *too much*, your credentials eventually reveal the truth and make you seem a bit delusional. Create an excellent portfolio before you apply for a job, and you don't fall short of expectations. Consider it comparable to creating a good product, first, and worrying about marketing it later.

Confidence means that you know that you do a good job for a studio, and you support your claims with facts. When asked how you handle the workload, you convey your faith in your ability to adapt to new challenges. When you lack faith in yourself, you reflect your doubt outwardly through your personality. People sense that something about you isn't right.

Cockiness, on the other hand, is unacceptable—unless you have an awesome reputation and over a decade of industry experience. The game industry values confident team players who don't brag about their talent.

17   Asking Questions

During an interview, don't ask run-of-the-mill questions. Throw your interviewers off guard with a provocative question applicable to their studio. The question-and-answer section at the end of an interview is your chance to show that you're interested enough in the position to think critically about your questions. When your interviewers run out of time answering your questions, it's a good thing.

Don't quietly respond, "I don't have any questions." When you don't ask questions, interviewers think you are uninterested or you're too shy.

Bring enough copies of your resume for your interviewers and for yourself. During the interview, quickly jot down key words on the back of your copy of your resume. Use the key words to recall your questions at the end of the interview. Ask as many questions as you can.

When you struggle to devise interesting questions, ask questions unrelated to your job, or ask questions you might find the answers to yourself. Asking those questions buys you time to think of unique and interesting questions.

18   Preparing to Move Immediately

When you apply to a studio over one thousand miles away, and the studio hires you, they might expect you to start the next week. Game professionals flaunt their experiences of leaving everything in another city to join a new studio. Some people continue paying rent on their previous apartments to finish their leases, and they move their belongings into self-storage units. These people are your competition, *and* they're experienced. Stay equally flexible to compete in this market.

A friend was asked during a phone interview how long he needed to relocate. He said that he could relocate immediately. During a phone interview, don't give a studio any inkling that you aren't the best candidate. Prepare to make sacrifices to win the position.

Job Search Examples

The section that follows includes examples of three phone interviews/initial screenings that I experienced with different development studios. All three began in February, which is typically a good month to hire. I was already employed by a studio, and I was casually perusing the job market.

This February occurred during one of the worst recessions in American history, proving that even when times get hard, you can find opportunities when you stay alert.

A studio in Seattle (*Griptonite Games*):

- An HR manager called me about a permanent position.
- The studio offered to reimburse relocation expenses.
- I didn't get past the first interview, because they asked whether I was ready to leave my current studio. I was honest, and I said that I wanted to wait to determine the fate of my contract position.

A studio in Oregon (*Bend Studio*):

- The producer and lead environment artist called for a three-way conversation after I innocently asked via a generic jobs email address whether the studio's website was current and whether the studio sought new employees.
- The studio had a one-year contract position open.
- The studio was unwilling to aid with relocation.

A studio in Seattle creating a popular space marine FPS (*343 Studios*)

- A staffing-agency employee contacted me about a one-year contract position.
- The studio was unwilling to reimburse relocation expenses, but offered to increase my current annual salary by $12,000.
- If the studio chose to pursue me for the position, they would arrange two interviews via *Skype* with the studio's developers.
- The studio wanted young, energetic people to help make quality projects. (A seasoned colleague translated this to mean that they wanted *people for crunch*.)
- A representative from the studio called to tell me they chose other candidates with more seniority.
- The staffing employee followed up to tell me that I was on the list for future new positions.

A studio in Dallas (*Terminal Reality*):

- The HR manager called, and our conversation was personal and less about job requirements.
- The studio had an available four- to six-month contract position.
- The studio was unwilling to reimburse relocation expenses.
- The HR manager was ready to end the conversation when I told her that I didn't live in Dallas, because she

assumed that I wouldn't relocate for a short-term position.

A studio in Dallas—Part 2, four months later:

- The HR manager called me to ask whether I found a job yet. Now, the studio was hiring full-time employees. I wasn't looking for new opportunities at the time, but she remembered me from our previous conversation. Maintaining a good relationship with a studio is invaluable.

A *very* well-known studio in San Diego (*Rockstar Games*):

- I applied for a position online, and I mentioned that a colleague worked at the studio, previously.
- The colleague put in a good word with the lead artist about my work ethic.
- The art director responded to my application for the full-time position via phone call.
- The studio would arrange my flight to San Diego for an in-person interview after an initial phone screening.
- The art director wanted an updated, *industry-work-only* portfolio, which I couldn't provide as a recent graduate.
- I didn't get far enough into the conversation to inquire about the salary.

A studio in Austin (*Certain Affinity*):

- A staffing agency emailed me. They must have found my online portfolio.
- The agency contacted me in November, which suggested that the studio was in crunch. Studios ramp games to ship for the holidays.
- The studio proposed a six-month contract with a chance of extension.
- The studio asked if I developed PC or console games, which tools I used, and whether I was interested in a *realistic, futuristic,* and *grungy* style.

19   Taking Art Tests

People might think that an art test before an interview is standard in the industry. However, arts test don't automatically follow applications. One hiring agency told an artist that studios issue art tests only when studios lack confidence in candidates' portfolios. When your portfolio clearly demonstrates your capabilities, studios might exempt you from art tests.

During art tests, artists should display different views of scenes to demonstrate skills beyond basic modeling, such as lighting, texturing, composition, environment layout, and level design. For designers and programmers, tests typically consist of question-and-answer sessions. Interviewers might describe a hypothetical task and ask you to list detailed steps about your approach to complete it. Interviewers might also ask you to define certain technical terminology.

20 Discovering What Studios *Really* Want

When I condense what studios desire in job candidates into five key ingredients, they are: **reputable work, potential to improve and excel, technical skills, genuine eagerness,** and **good cultural fit.** The following section is an abridged version of advice from hiring departments.

Often, websites post jobs with lifeless, sterile requirements and descriptions. The best way to determine what a studio wants is to ask. Learning what studios want also gives you job security. Ask what to do and what to avoid, and your boss will be happy that you play by the rules.

A core group of leaders determines each studio's desired environment. Each studio is vastly different in strategy, but core values are usually similar:

- Make the best games possible within the given limitations.
- Work as little crunch as possible.
- Hire the best in the business.

When you put yourself into the shoes of a studio leader, you discover that these checkpoints are more easily said than done. Most layoffs create opportunities for studios to correct previous hiring mistakes.

When you provide quality output according to the studio's definition, don't sweat the small stuff. Maintain skills comparable to current industry expectations, and keep your network large and friendly. That's your best job security.

Personality goes hand-in-hand with skill. Some employees with unpleasant personalities provide exemplary work, and some people with infectious personalities provide only mediocre work. Most studios have enough of the former. Newcomers with enthusiastic personalities are more employable than employees who are more technically skilled but difficult to work with. The industry needs young and enthusiastic game developers to revive the jaded veterans and put in the hours necessary to ship a title on time.

An experienced freelance artist in Los Angeles said that the most talented artists in the business are usually the cockiest, and nobody wants to deal with them. They are similar to basketball stars hogging the ball, earning resentment from their teams who'd do better without them.

It is easier for studios to hire candidates who fit the company culture than to hire applicants who don't match, and then force the culture down their throats. Employees who cooperate are more valuable than uninteresting people with skills, because projects are bigger than ever and require better collaboration. Thus, most employees at a given studio have compatible personalities, senses of humor, and styles of dress. When you get the impression that you're incompatible, your intuition foretells potential problems down the line. Wildly opposing personalities cause conflict. Employees at game studios act casually, and you must deal with their good, bad, and *ugly* sides.

Provide solutions to problems; don't just point them out. Don't be a complainer. Often, you can solve a problem over a two-minute conversation with someone in another department. In a studio, you have plenty of resources. When you can't find someone to help you with a specific problem, search for the answer online. Valuable team members show initiative to learn the studio's tools and improve processes.

Near the end of a project, studios focus on fixing bugs. Fixing bugs is purely troubleshooting and problem solving. It is hardly creative or collaborative. Chances are, a newcomer might receive a job offer during crunch or near the end of a project. The studio expects you to solve problems quickly, and you don't have time to meet people or form relationships. Studios expect compliance during this period. Prove yourself through your talent. During crunch, studios aren't interested in your stellar personality. When an intern asked a lead what he looks for in a good employee, the lead said that his priorities for a good intern include the following:

- Potential
- Personality
- Skill

Obviously, interns shouldn't ruffle feathers or cause trouble. Interns are learning, and they don't complete assignments perfectly. That's okay. Speed, unfortunately, is often stressed over quality. When you produce useable content at a rapid speed, you are valuable. Interns might complete cleanup tasks, such as error-proofing files and fixing small issues that help other people complete important tasks. These tasks don't require perfection, because they're less visible aspects of a game.

An artist's work should have the following characteristics:

- Cleanliness
- Functionality in game
- Consistency with the game's style
- Quick to craft

Believe in yourself. Think big. Don't be afraid of failure. Go the extra mile. This advice is timeless. People always find new and tempting ways of doing more with less and achieving success without trying. However, the same basic advice that's proven valuable through the ages still applies today. Society seems bored with it, though, and people prefer to believe the beautiful lies. Flashy, innovative advice is enticing because it sounds easy.

A senior designer at a AAA studio recommends the following advice about what studios look for in their employees:

1. The most important part about being a game designer is convincing at least fifteen people—a design team—to like your idea. A quiet programmer might have a good idea, but when he doesn't fight for it, the studio never implements it.

2. Game designers must learn to do only the tasks their bosses want. They must avoid taking games in other

directions. Unless you're a lead, coworkers don't whole-heartedly trust your ideas; you're expected to contribute to achieving someone else's vision.

3. When you and your manager share the same work ethic, you come out okay. When your manager spends more time working than you do, he or she doesn't like you, thinking you're a slacker. When you work more hours than your manager, you dislike your manager. Try arriving and departing the office around the same time as your lead.

4. You should be happy, even when you don't completely enjoy what you do. When you develop games for as many hours we do, you *should* enjoy it (to stay sane).

IV. STAYING EMPLOYED

1   Cutting Your Teeth

Your first position is probably the least glamorous of your career. You learn new procedures or processes, such as creating collision for art that players never see, troubleshooting files, or error-proofing components that players never notice.

Although the assignments aren't glamorous, don't cross the line into the dangerous territory of performing office errands, such as fetching coffee. Impressing your boss is wise, but a better way to impress is to request additional assignments, and do them well. When your boss tries to use you as a personal assistant—this doesn't apply to producers—explain that you're more useful completing the tasks the studio hired you to do. Tedious tasks are part of development, and bosses don't object to additional contributions.

Don't complain about your assignments immediately after you start working at a studio; complaining might insult your boss. For example, a new designer in her first entry-level position shouldn't expect to change the entire story of a game. When you frequently complain, your boss might even assign you unpleasant tasks to teach you about respect.

Candidates searching for jobs often consider the type of games that studios produce first, and they consider studios' locations second. Few job seekers—especially those new to the industry—consider studios' working environments. They'd rather work for the popular big-budget studios, and they don't think about the long hours those studios require. Finding a job in a company with a culture congruent with your own personality is important.

How do you research a studio's culture before accepting a position there? Culture is obviously more difficult to research than researching which games a studio produces. To assess a studio's culture, talk with employees at the studio. Ask for secondhand information from a friend of a studio employee, or ask HR managers at job fairs. These three separate sources might differ in candor, so read between the lines. For instance, consider a studio losing talented employees because of excessive crunch. That studio is likely to crunch the same amount on future projects. Startups are an exception, because a startup's first project is proving grounds for its reputation.

You can also gauge a company's culture by attending company parties and getting to know its employees. You can learn a lot observing the style of a party. Is the party upscale and pretentious? Do employees socialize in larger groups, or do they stand around, trying to look cool?

Public relations advertising displayed at career events also helps you gauge a company's culture. The PR might include a 2D still-image advertisement, or maybe it includes a short video. Does the studio take itself too seriously, or is it immature? The way representatives dress and talk at job fair booths reveals how the studio operates. When a studio sends only quiet HR employees—not developers—the studio doesn't care much about recruiting. Or, perhaps its developers endure excessive overtime, and they have no time to attend job fairs.

My friend told me a story about approaching a AAA studio's booth at GDC. He didn't make an appointment in advance. He approached a woman at the studio's front desk. She told him that the developers wouldn't talk with anyone without an appointment, because they were busy. My friend told her that answering his question would take only take a minute; he didn't intend to bug them about a job. He essentially requested an informational interview. She denied his request, and she gave him a condescending look that suggested he shouldn't have come in the first place.

Understandably, event hosts deal with masses of job seekers approaching their booths with varying levels of politeness; they can't entertain everyone, simultaneously. However, this condescending attitude sends a message that studio employees' egos are larger than life. Even music superstars make time to sign autographs for eager fans. Sure, big studios produce quality games, but it might be hard to get along with a big studio's team unless you share the same attitude.

The same studio hosted a haughty party that year. Attendees didn't talk with each other. It was a coolness competition. The studio spent a ton of money on this *invite-only* party featuring belly dancers, a laser-light show, upscale decorations, and fancy hors d'oeuvres. The party said a lot about the culture of that studio.

2   Fulfilling Expectations

Stay on good terms with your studio by following your lead's priorities, not your own. When you put your priorities above your manager's, your manager worries that you don't contribute enough. She might question your performance, because neglecting your assignments reflects poorly on you.

When perfectionism drives you to fix every little detail, remember that the only details that matter to your success are the ones determined by your lead. For example, when you notice a problem the lead overlooked, don't escalate that issue until you complete your assignment. Your priority is fixing glaring issues, and then you can revisit the small, quick fixes.

To maximize efficiency, environment artists should apply the environment textures, and UV map them first. UV mapping is a process of arranging surface details to create a 3D model's color and form. Add finer details later, such as adding scary storytelling elements for a haunted environment or placing little footprints on the ground of an old corridor. Complete your tasks, and other departments can begin theirs. When you apply the textures to the art, a texture artist—when applicable—unifies the textures to make them more rich and convincing.

Take thorough notes during critiques from your lead, because you should fix all the issues before the next review. The lead knows when something on her mental list wasn't completed. By taking notes, you create a clear checklist. Use the notes to remind you to give every item your ample attention. Forgetting to complete a handful of tasks because you don't take notes is a waste of time. A senior designer said that he doesn't trust anyone who doesn't take notes to get the job done the first time. He expects people without notes to return with questions about what he already covered.

Time estimates are crucial to schedule project workload. Track your hours on side projects and mini-tasks at home. To improve labor time estimates, practice by recording how long you spend on personal work. Studios expect you to accurately estimate your speed when you start your first task. Estimating is an essential skill that many applicants overlook. Few advisors tell new applicants to learn how to estimate before they enter production environments.

You should always add contingency time to your estimates, because distractions and complications inevitably arise. When your boss tells you specifically not to pad your estimates, you should make a conservative estimate to allow enough time. Completing tasks early looks better than readjusting schedules for unanticipated hardships. After you complete your tasks, your boss passes the project to another department. When you complete the task ahead of schedule, other departments potentially get ahead. And you look like a rockstar when you finish a task before the estimated time.

Sometimes studios assign producers to departments to help team members organize schedules and to monitor employees' estimates. Current technologies with online capabilities, such as *Hansoft*, remove the guesswork of estimates.

3   Practicing File-Management Etiquette

Most studios use the file-handling client *Perforce*, *which* is an online platform that allows employees to update their files and share their changes with the rest of the studio. Employees may begin working where another employee left off. Studios might not share the unspoken rules about file management, but they certainly hold you accountable to follow them. Here are the basics:

1. Do not leave files checked out overnight. Other team members might stay later at the office or arrive earlier, and they require access to the files. When you suddenly become sick or win the lottery, they can't fix an emergency bug in your file because you've got it checked out. When the build is majorly broken and the problem is in your file, keeping the file checked out prevents other departments from troubleshooting the problem.

2. When you check out a file, you reserve the exclusive right to update it; other team members can't make changes. When you suspect that someone else might need that file soon, make only the most important changes, and check in the file quickly.

3. When a coworker is modifying a shared file, and you're not sure what he or she is doing, politely instant message, email, or ask in person if your coworker plans to check in the changes. Then, wait until that person gives you the cue that the file is ready before you modify it. When your coworker responds that he or she is using that file, you must wait until the coworker checks it in before you modify it.

4   Preparing for a Sea of Cynics

The game industry embraces the best collection of people from different disciplines coming together to make something great. Period. With this in mind, you might imagine studio employees are happy, motivated, and know how to have fun. After all, it takes fun people to make fun games, right?

Game development is repetitive and mindless at times. Maybe the region of the game assigned to you is not your favorite. The "teeth-cutting" period is longer now than it used to be, which makes talented new video game developers desperate to produce more compelling work.

Being cynical is a lifestyle. Game industry professionals were probably cynical *before* they joined the industry. Most studios don't want to hire cynics. HR reps and leads say this repeatedly. Yet, many aspiring game developers have cynical mindsets. They hide cynicism during interviews, but the attitudes emerge quickly after they start new jobs. Studios seek candidates with positive attitudes who don't complain, who are humble, and who get results. If you're cynical by nature, read personal development books to help you develop a more caring and enthusiastic personality.

Understanding the difference between cynicism and criticism is crucial to becoming a better employee. When you're told that you are wrong, even when the message is rudely delivered, the message might be intended to help you correct a problem. The worst criticism is no criticism, so rude criticism is better than none. People who struggle to make it into the industry might falter because they can't handle criticism. The products from a developer who shies away from criticism are inferior to those of developers embracing criticism to improve.

You can choose between the following ways to deal with criticism:

1. You can continue working and ignore it.

2. You can think deeply, assume the criticism stems from genuinely good intentions, and revise your work accordingly.

Obviously, the second choice is more productive. However, you should dismiss unhelpful criticism. When criticism insults you personally or doesn't intend to help, it might be considered discrimination. You don't need to deal with discrimination. Human resources departments exist to address these issues. If you're a victim, consult HR. Keep your business community respectful.

5   Getting a Side Job Quickly to Pay the Bills

You might need a temporary side job during an unsustainable employment gap. Managers of small companies usually want long-term employees, yet few people actually hold these jobs for long. Most video game professionals don't want to flip burgers for more than a few months—tops.

The following procedure to land a part-time job comes from a friend, a master of switching part-time jobs who changed positions every couple of months. This tactic works best when an employer is actively hiring, so check job postings and "now-hiring" signs beforehand.

1. Complete an application. Make it clean, organized, and use perfect grammar. Attach your resume.

2. Arrive—in person—with your completed application, ask to talk with a manager, and hand the manager your application. Tell the manager your name, and provide quick background information about why you're appropriate for the position. Don't provide unnecessary detail. Make it quick and energetic; a fleeting introduction leaves the manager wanting more.

3. Two days later, call and ask for the manager. Request an update on the status of your application. Ask to speak with the person you met when you applied.

4. During your interview, don't lie, but sweeten the truth by telling the manager that you plan to stay for "as long as possible." Don't divulge exact dates. Don't mention your plans to return to the video game industry.

5. Request the hiring manager's email address, and send a thank-you email.

This strategy doesn't work in professional industries where your resume and portfolio come into play. Use the application methods listed in this book for professional industries.

6   Finding a Job Is Easier When You Already Have One

When I searched for studios jobs, I noticed how it was exponentially easier to spark a potential employer's interest when I already had a job. When I didn't have a job, studios didn't respond to my emails. Rejections took forever—when they came at all. When I had a job, and I casually browsed for new opportunities, I encountered several studios interested in hiring me.

The more prominent your current studio, the more other studios desire you. Your current position indicates that you are valuable. Your current studio presumably keeps you employed because of your great performance.

You should always seek new opportunities. Maintain a backup plan in case something unfortunate happens at your studio. Conducting interviews with other studios and entertaining job offers isn't cheating on your current studio; it's required. If you lose your job, you need relationships lined up with other studios that might have job openings.

The downside of "jumping" studios is that "nobody likes a jumper," according to Cliff Bleszinski. "Stay with your current studio for a couple of years before moving to another."

Build a reputation with each studio, and be an asset. If you move from studio to studio, do so on good terms. Don't leave right before you finish a project. Studios expect freelancers to jump studios, but full-time employees should think twice.

Contrarily, if you approach a studio after getting laid off, the studio might wonder what you did wrong. It's unfair that people with opportunities are granted more opportunities, but use this to your advantage by improving your situation when times are good.

7   Finding a Cheap Place to Stay

When you accept a job offer in a new, unfamiliar location, finding housing before your first day at a new job can be stressful. Most people find apartments near a studio and pay high rent for a short-term lease. Many game industry jobs are contract-based, typically with six- to twelve-month contracts. Most apartment leases are nine months to one year. They typically charge higher rent for shorter contracts, and they penalize tenants for breaking a lease early. Avoid apartment leases when you want to save money.

First, find an area near the office where you can save money by walking or biking to the office. Use a rooms-for-rent website like craigslist.org or HotPads.com instead of leasing an apartment. Look for a month-to-month contract that's less expensive than an apartment with fewer obligations. I recommend using the website PadMapper.com. The website includes real-time craigslist.org postings based on map locations. You can find the best price *and* the best location.

I used this strategy to find an inexpensive room near my first game studio. I found a tiny room advertised on craigslist.org for $385 monthly, plus utilities, in a house shared by five men.

Some people prefer a private space. Because I lived in a small house with several housemates, I visited my girlfriend's place for privacy. Because I mainly used the room to sleep—we were crunching at the time—it was a perfect match. Two years later, I saved enough money to mortgage a house. I couldn't have saved for a down payment if I had leased a fancy apartment and spent over half of my paycheck on rent. Yet, most people choose that route.

8   Working Abroad

Ditch your parents. Choose a school far from your hometown, and develop independence. When you're unemployed, find cheap housing before resorting to returning to the nest. Supporting yourself motivates you, because you *must* succeed to live. When you're not living in your parents' house, you can build your portfolio as long as you want and as late as you want—without anyone telling you to sleep more or stop working so much. Living alone also develops your self-discipline and improves your work habits. These traits transform you into a valuable employee.

Jack Mamais, the former lead designer at Crytek and an American living in Germany, revealed an aspect he dislikes about the video game industry: Moving abroad in search of employment. He said that he doesn't consider long-term arrangements such as leasing an apartment or renting a house. He purchases lightweight, easy-to-move furniture, and he's always ready for his next move.

An art director said he has never bought a house, because he's never found a way to own a house with a career in the video game industry. He laughed at the idea of owning a home, and said he'd love to find a good solution.

Recently, that art director bought a house in a city with a lower cost of living. He remained at the same studio for a few years before making that commitment, though.

You shouldn't buy a house when you plan to move in the next few years. The industry is volatile, so most video game professionals avoid home ownership. A character rigger in the U.S. bought a house before pursuing an opportunity in Finland one year later. He had to repay a first-time homebuyer's credit of $8000 because he sold the home immediately after buying it. He also had to find renters for his house to pay the next month's mortgage while he searched for a buyer. He was expecting a child with his spouse at the time, and the situation stressed the family.

Some locations have less viable housing markets, let alone affordable apartment housing. A volunteer program coordinator at GDC confirmed that most San Franciscans share apartments to afford the high cost of living.

Another friend in New York pays a considerable chunk of his monthly salary—$1,400—to rent a closet-sized space in a three-bedroom condo he shares with two roommates. Although his pay is slightly higher than colleagues' in other cities—$70,000/year—he lives paycheck to paycheck because of New York's high cost of living.

The following section describes the cost of living in various regions of the U.S., and notes how living in these areas might affect your career planning:

The West Coast

A senior graphics programmer at a studio in Austin said, "Most people doing high-end work are getting out of California [where most of the high-end studios are, and have been since the creation of video games]. It's just too expensive."

Dreams of participating in this "super fun" industry in expensive places, like California, ring hollow in times of economic stress. The California lifestyle is less sustainable than others. California is like a playground for adults, but at a cost. Housing prices are astronomical. To rent a house on a single income with enough money remaining for decent savings, people commute over an hour from homes outside major cities. The climate and natural environment are beautiful, but people can't enjoy them from the inside of dark offices all day—especially when a studio requires excessive overtime.

A professor told stories about former students working in big cities, particularly Los Angeles. He said they commute an hour or two via carpool and share housing with two or three coworkers.

Texas

Prepare to earn a lower salary in the Lone Star State. But, you get a virtual raise, because Texas currently collects no state income taxes. Texas' lower cost of living also justifies earning smaller salaries. Texas is a right-to-work state, which means employers can terminate employees without warning—even full-time, salaried employees. When you work in Texas, don't do anything stupid, such as irritating the wrong person.

The Midwest—Iowa, Illinois, and Wisconsin

When you move to the Midwest, prepare for the long haul. Studios relocating employees to the Midwest aren't planning to fire them anytime soon. Studios have a hard time enticing job candidates to move to these areas isolated from the rest of the industry. Midwestern professionals risk losing their jobs with fewer opportunities to get back on their feet quickly.

A junior employee at Volition shared his experience living in a small, desolate town. Although lacking in fun, both the cost of living and salaries are lower. These cities are slower-paced with fewer activities.

9   Considering Job Titles

Most people imagine progressing to higher positions throughout their careers. Sometimes professionals move laterally, or even down the ladder. Most senior-level employees must settle for mid-level positions when they change studios. Accepting a lower-level position is especially troublesome for professionals with many years of experience who lose jobs when games get canceled. Some studios measure seniority based on the number of shipped titles on your resume, so a canceled project impacts years of your career.

Different studios use different tiers of titles. When you are *junior-level three*, you expect a promotion to *mid-level one*. However, when you move to another studio, the new studio might hire you at *junior-level one*. Another studio might not use a tiered system. That studio might propel you to a *mid-level* position.

Some studios divide the tasks of managing employees and managing quality—creating the *lead* and *principal* positions. *Leads* manage schedules to ensure team members are tasked correctly and motivated.

Principals have the skills required to develop the game, and they actively touch the same content as senior-level employees. Principals communicate with other departments and aid lower-level employees. Note that not all studios employ this specific position.

Employees who prefer to hone their talents tend to choose the principal role. They feel that leads are less talented, because they don't practice their skills on the job.

A top-level art director said, "Everyone wants to be an art director, but nobody has a good reason to want it."

Don't aim too high right out of school. Conveying an overly ambitious attitude suggests naiveté. When you can't explain your goals, you appear delusional. Instead of boasting about your career expectations, hint at them. Demonstrate your value, first. When people see your output, they admire your commitment to your success.

When you repeatedly demonstrate characteristics of your future self, your future success becomes imminent in the minds of people around you. Instead of explicitly stating your objectives, reveal them implicitly. Cooperate with people instead of competing against them. Gain their respect, and prove your talent.

V. CAREER PROGRESSION

1   Meeting Higher Expectations

Articulate your goals, and hold yourself accountable for your progress. At professional studios, you receive progress reports with feedback about your performance. You're expected to set your personal goals. Working toward your goals helps you prove your value to the organization and track your progress, simultaneously.

Take progress reports and goals seriously. Some people aren't interested in improvement, and they set half-hearted goals. When you want to get ahead faster, determine the attributes you must develop to get there. You might have an opportunity to improve a skill, a personality trait, or a physical capability. Your leads notice your diligence and dedication to the studio. By continuously improving, you differentiate yourself from the crowd.

You might be tempted to interact with your lead as much as possible to get noticed. You want to show that you're an eager candidate, and you volunteer to do more. Contrarily, let your lead breathe, and give him or her space. In fact, you can impress your lead more by working cleanly and efficiently. Update your lead daily about your progress, but don't waste your lead's time asking about every little thing. You're independent. Leads are busy, and they're balancing many important priorities. You want to be the employee who gets things done quickly without much help—not the employee who asks the same questions repeatedly. Be self-sufficient. When you do sincerely have a question, ask your team members before approaching the lead. Leads expect higher-level employees to be more independent than everyone else.

2   Getting Noticed

One intern ended her file descriptions with two exclamation marks. Some coworkers thought it was funny, and others teased her about it—but she got noticed. The studio hired her full-time when her internship ended. The studio didn't hire her just because of the two exclamation marks, but it didn't hurt to set herself apart. The intern was also married to a studio employee, which was more influential than her punctuation.

Bring your boss gifts. A seasoned animator said, "You want to know how to get ahead in this industry? Bring your lead breakfast tacos!" He said it in front of the lead, so it was probably a joke. But, he brought breakfast tacos, nonetheless.

Employees might assume that gifts are kissing up. However, when you go out of your way often enough, you and your boss might get used to it. When your boss doesn't decline your gifts, they're working. I haven't tried this myself, but apparently, it works.

One morning, a mid-level animator catered breakfast tacos as a token of his appreciation for our entire team. Buying tacos for the entire team was an expensive gesture, and it was generous and thoughtful. The scale of his generosity seemed almost desperate, so maybe he was trying to gain respect. It surely got him noticed.

Another coworker regularly baked fresh banana bread for morning snacks. The team quickly gobbled up that bread, and banana bread became the coworker's trademark.

One more colleague brewed beer and hosted beer tastings on acceptable beer-drinking days. Sharing hobbies helps you stand out among your colleagues.

3   Forming Relationships During Downtimes

In a world controlled by computers, it is increasingly easier to avoid face-to-face conversations. Communicating through text feels distant, and people prefer feeling loved and special. Focusing only on work without connecting on a personal level makes you forgettable. Avoiding friendships also makes the office less fun for everyone.

Stop at your coworkers' desks every other day; keep up with their lives and their roles. When you work in a big studio, it may be fine to visit only your own team if the other teams are inconveniently far away. This technique is ridiculously effective to make others feel special. I certainly feel special when a coworker comes to my desk to ask questions about me. Personalized questions show that you care about your coworkers, and you're interested in their lives. If your coworkers wanted to work with a lifeless robot, they would outsource your job.

The more you keep up with people, the more they want to keep up with you. Then you become the most popular team member in the studio, and everyone is happy!

Be extra courteous and friendly to colleagues who help resolve problems you encounter. For example, designers should stay on good terms with programmers, and artists should stay on good terms with tech artists. These resources can save you from technical problems in a pinch. When you bug them unnecessarily, rub them the wrong way, or act rudely, they might brush you off and decline to help. A problem one particular coworker could solve in five minutes might take you hours to resolve, when you solve it at all. Remember what you learn from your coworkers, so you don't require help for the same issues repeatedly.

Building strong relationships takes time. You earn trust—people don't freely distribute it. Stay reserved when you start at a studio. Spend the first couple of weeks absorbing your environment. After you learn what's acceptable at the studio, you get more comfortable and act more openly.

4   Asking Rockstars

To learn the culture and expectations of a studio, ask one of its *rockstars*. A rockstar is an admirable employee with a good track record at the studio. Rockstars can help you deal with various situations. Consider a rockstar's advice as informal mentoring. When you encounter a problem, grab a rockstar for an informal meeting, and ask away (this is best done behind closed doors)!

When the rockstar is generous, he or she helps you. When you ask objective questions and avoid complaining, rockstars appreciate that you asked them for help. When you don't feel closure based on the rockstar's advice, climb the chain of command to your lead and head manager, if necessary. Most problems don't require the head manager's intervention, though.

5   Making Questions Your Weapons

"The intelligent person is the one who knows how to ask the right questions."

—Unknown

A coworker called me "Larry King" because I asked in-depth questions. Life is too short to restrict your conversation to the weather or mindless topics, in my opinion. We should all learn from each other to improve. You should still shoot the breeze, occasionally, because people naturally want to relax sometimes without answering tough questions.

Some powerhouse companies, like Toyota Motor Company, assign impossible tasks to new employees to gauge their ability to collaborate with others.[20] Many minds are better than one, and no one knows everything. This example proves you shouldn't feel ashamed or allow pride to prevent you from asking for help. Studios *want* you to ask your coworkers questions.

---

20. Liker, Jeffrey K., *The Toyota Way: 14 Management Principles from the World's Greatest Manufacturer*. New York: McGraw-Hill, 2004.

6   Applying Subliminal Techniques

Subliminal techniques might seem trivial, but when you implement subliminal techniques, you improve your chances of impressing people.

Post a picture of your kids on your desktop. You aren't a robot, and your managers think twice before firing you when they consider your family obligations.

Decorate your desk with items from home. Customize your space with objects that represent you. Your personal items show coworkers that you're comfortable being yourself in the office. Plus, after you've moved in, your desk is harder to clear or relocate. Removing your belongings might create a spectacle if you got laid off.

7   Going Full-Time from a Contract or Internship

I've struggled with this goal for a long time. Virtually no information exists online about becoming a full-time employee from a contract position—especially in the game industry.

I recommend you invite your manager to lunch to discuss your opportunities. Develop a relationship prior to the invitation, which takes planning. An art director mentioned after each meeting that he and I should go out to lunch, which was a direct invitation. He eventually offered a specific invitation.

A lead advised me that, "Being valuable is all about paying attention."

Pay attention to ways you might work better or faster, and execute them. Pay attention to process flaws, and correct them. The more you practice, keep an open mind, and pay attention, the more you improve.

Don't fall in love with your work. When you finish your job, your content might get cut or changed completely. Especially starting out, recognize that you provide a service to your director. When your director doesn't want something you've created in the game, remove it. Aspects of a game getting cut don't indicate a failure on your part; you helped the director see them in-game, and he or she decided that they didn't fit. Keep your eye on the overall strategy, and don't selfishly believe that your opinion is more important than your boss's. This takes some getting used to, especially for rookies.

8   Staying Focused

Get a great set of headphones. When you face a tight deadline and your neighbor chatters nonstop, it's annoying and distracting. When you wear your headphones, you send a polite signal that you're busy, and you don't appreciate unimportant interruptions.

Respect the headphones; it's an unwritten code. If your studio doesn't provide headphones, go buy some. The bigger your headphones, the better. Coworkers don't bother you when they notice your headphones from far away, but they might overlook your in-ear headphones.

Try the one-ear headphone technique. Place your headphones over one ear, like a cool DJ at a trendy club. The one-ear technique allows you to listen to music or audiobooks, but you can still hear your boss or colleagues calling your name or discussing something important to you.

Use your email program as a personal assistant. Configure an alert for emails sent to you directly. Those emails are probably more urgent than emails addressed to the entire company. Create a saved folder for your most important emails, so you're never at a loss for information. You never know when a tip you received six months ago might come in handy.

Create a folder for automated emails, such as build information or automated IT updates. At one studio, admins sent build emails every time tasks went to the build machine, when builds finished, etc. I created a folder named "Build," and added a rule to check for the word "build" in the email title. Those emails filtered into the folder. Build emails didn't require my immediate response, so I deleted the messages in one swoop when the folder got full. This automation avoided daily distractions from unimportant email alerts.

Document your contributions. When you depend on someone else to finish something for you, send an email instead of an instant message. Coworkers sometimes forget instant message conversations, but emails provide hard evidence that you sent your request. When you want to use an instant messenger as an informal, quicker, and more natural way to communicate, send an email afterward to summarize your chat discussion. Summaries also help your coworkers, because they can store your messages in saved folders, highlight them, and look for them later.

9   Losing Your Contract Position

Previous sections of this book address keeping your developer job. You've learned about what *to do*; now learn what *not to do*. This section provides surefire ways to lose your job. I witnessed these examples of subsequently terminated employees. Avoid these activities unless you truly want to get fired.

Spend excessive time browsing mindless websites.

Posting on social networking sites while you submit your work late or riddled with errors sends the message that you don't care about quality. Bystanders notice when you're posting or chatting about non-work topics and generally slacking off while they're working. Eventually, your boss might catch you, and bad habits don't work in your favor. Even if you browse the Internet only moderately at the office, when you happen to make a mistake in your work, coworkers might blame you for using your computer resources for entertainment purposes.

Be forgettable.

When people don't know you, you're forgettable. People don't care when forgettable people get laid off. When a senior department member doesn't know the name of an employee who's worked there for over six months, that person is at risk. Don't be that person.

Take vacation during crunch.

Crunch is absolutely the worst time to take vacation, because crunch is when the studio needs you most. Coworkers depend on you. Every warm body eases the burden. Most contractors aren't eligible for vacation time in the first place. But sometimes, studios make exceptions. Employees who take time off on short notice during crunch usually find themselves unemployed— unless their reputations are unbeatable.

Avoid crunch.

Most studios don't volunteer the subject of crunch, but most consider it unavoidable. Some studios prevent crunch, which is a sign of maturation in the industry. When you're new to the industry, studios expect you to work the longest hours of your career. You might have to work crunch during your entire first contract position.

Some employees rebel against long hours. An employee at one studio claimed the long hours were unfair. He suggested the studio managers "forced" employees to work without overtime pay. That employee tried to recruit others to join his rally, and he sent a letter to the contract agency that paid the employees. The contract agency contacted the studio's HR department about his claims, and the HR department fired that vigilante immediately. Shamefully, few industry professionals come forward about the long hours, possibly out of fear for losing their jobs or tarnishing their reputations.

The studio never mentioned the employee's departure, and many coworkers didn't realize he left. He was forgettable. The moral of the story is that crunch is undesirable, but average employees don't change the way studios handle crunch. If you're against crunch, find a studio that crunches less. Understandably, most people don't object to crunch when contributing to big name titles. They want their names in the credits.

10 Gauging Your Performance

Smaller studios don't always provide much direction in the personal development realm. Communication might be limited, and you might receive little feedback about your performance. Working as a contractor or intern amplifies this lack of feedback. Even more disheartening, you receive feedback when you flounder, but not when you thrive.

A veteran artist said that when your boss doesn't reprimand you, you're on the right track. Essentially, lack of disciplinary action *is* the positive feedback. This varies from studio to studio, and feedback about your performance depends on your leader's management style. Some leaders generously dole out the positive reinforcement, while others may not say anything at all.

There are subtle ways to discern your manager's perceptions about you. For example, I wanted to take time off to volunteer at GDC. I was a contractor then, and I approached the art director to request time off. She was suspicious about my request to attend the conference, joking, "I hope you're not going to get a new job, because we need you here!"

Her reaction signaled that she considered me valuable. Later, the studio art director (higher up in the organization than the art director) discussed plans for the studio. She told me, "Don't leave for at least two more years!" Two years was the remainder of the project.

Both of these examples sent clear signals that I had a strong chance of getting hired after the term of my contract. I was correct in my assumption, and the studio offered me a full-time position shortly thereafter.

11   Requesting a Raise

An HR manager told me that HR employees typically don't approve pay increases without first consulting your manager(s). Additionally, some studios adhere to strict pay ranges for each title. Your title might limit your opportunities for a pay raise. To overcome those limitations, you must earn a promotion.

To earn a promotion, talk with a lead or director. Approach the topic politely and professionally, and ask specifically what is required for a higher position. Collaborate with your lead to develop goals to reach the next level.

Your attitude should be, "I will do everything possible to make this happen! I want to be the best possible employee for this company."

Meet with your lead monthly to track the progress of your goals. You might not be eligible for a promotion until you gain enough experience for the new position, but experience requirements are *usually* negotiable. The studio might have to file paperwork through its corporate office or publisher to move you to a new salary bracket. Some studios grant only a small number of promotions studio-wide, so your leader might have to wrestle against other departments to convince them to promote you.

Other studios are informal about their approaches to promotions and raises. Earning a promotion is the noblest way to earn a raise. Don't expect a huge raise, unless your game development is phenomenal. Even with phenomenal talent, studios don't award raises until employees request them.

There are notable exceptions to these guidelines:

- An entry-level environment artist earned a promotion to character artist because his work and reputation at the studio were so treasured by the art director. He was also a close relative to one of the top studio directors. The art director asked him to name a desired salary for his promotion.
- A well-known veteran of the industrial design field— not quite the same, but similar to video games—

worked for Oakley, the major sporty brand of sunglasses. Oakley considered him an indispensable employee, and he had worked in that industry forever. So, Oakley reportedly asked him to write a figure on a piece of paper, and said they'd consider it his new salary—no questions asked!

Those are exceptions. Unless you're a lucky rockstar, don't expect that kind of treatment. Raises are more formulaic, and they take more time for the average game developer.

12   Managing Your Expectations

Don't storm into the video game industry expecting to get rich right out of the gate. Research salary information using websites like SimplyHired.com and PayScale.com or refer to *Game Developer* magazine's Annual Salary Survey. Average game development salaries are modest. The game industry's appeal is fame—not fortune, as developers joke. Developers can earn a decent living. You find opportunities through persistence and willingness to try responsible—thus undesirable—roles.

Demanding candidates negotiate their salaries before joining their first studios, while others avoid negotiation. Sharpen your negotiation skills early in your career. Negotiation is an essential life skill that becomes more important throughout your life.

Don't list your previous salaries on job applications, and encourage your interviewer to initiate a salary offer. These techniques get difficult when studios request your previous salary during your initial phone screen. Avoid sharing the information, if possible, and change the subject. Suggest that you prefer to reach an agreement without discussing your previous pay. Instead, you prefer to evaluate your actual value to the company.

A colleague moved to California where salaries are higher, and he inflated his previous salary on his application by $15,000. His deceit worked. The HR rep didn't verify his previous salary. However, dishonesty is immoral, and liars eventually get caught.

In fact, the best way to get a raise in salary is by switching studios. Career advice websites indicate that employees sometimes change employers for noticeable promotions, particularly among large corporations. If you stay at your current studio, seniority will be the main basis in receiving promotions, no matter how hard you work. If you want to advance based on your work ethic and proactivity, your chances are better at a smaller studio.

If you create the greatest game ever—the game so great that mortals are unworthy to play it—you won't stay in business for long. This destructive thinking is rampant across the industry. Only a few role-model employees that studios send to conferences actually deal with fans, address the media, and represent the company in public. Others probably don't want to attend conferences, because they are shy and don't care to appease fans with small talk. The industry can only hope to improve relationships with its fans when it learns to employ compassion.

Some game professionals can't handle fame. When employees of a popular studio wear company gear in public, people ask questions about the company or its games. Developers might dishonestly suggest that they are merely fans, themselves, not employees. They avoid involvement with their audiences, the fans who make their games popular. Power brings responsibility. When developers don't want fans to approach them, they shouldn't publicly flaunt their company swag.

VI. THE BUSINESS

Video game developers use the following milestones to describe projects:

1. Concept
2. Preproduction
3. Production
4. Content complete
5. Pre-alpha
6. Alpha
7. Beta
8. Gold

Alpha describes the milestone when players may progress through the game from start to finish. Of the development phases, alpha usually involves the most crunch. *Gold* means the game is ready to release and ship to the public.

Production leads divide the major phases with smaller milestones. When a director deems one department's contribution unsatisfactory, the studio misses that scheduled milestone. Employees must scramble to complete makeup work to reach a passable state before the next scheduled milestone.

During the concept and preproduction phases of a project, developers schedule high-level game production milestones and pitch them to the publishers for approval.

Publishers either accept proposed schedules or reduce the time allotted. Publishers rarely add time to proposed schedules. Studios routinely follow biweekly scheduled milestones. Studios promise accomplishments to the publishers, called deliverables. Deliverables usually include neatly designed packages of levels, features, and art. These regular deliveries to publishers report the updated development progress. Publishers use deliverables to gauge quality and ensure studios fulfill commitments to finish games on time.

Some publishers pay bonuses when studios successfully meet scheduled milestones. Studios typically distribute these bonuses to their full-time developers. Contrarily, when studios fail consecutive milestones, publishers raise eyebrows. To compensate for an extended production time, publishers consider eliminating staff to reduce cost.

1   Coordinating With Outsourcing Vendors

Although I've written this section from an artist's point of view, outsourcing affects all departments. Output from outsourcing firms is unpredictable—especially with communication barriers. Studio employees working with outsourcing firms are challenged to identify the sources of outsourcer failures. Outsourcing vendors typically receive training from studios prior to taking on assignments. Reverse-engineering processes to detect the root causes of outsourcing blunders might require full-time commitments of studio employees.

When you partner with outsourcing firms, find a universal communication style understood by non-English speaking countries, if necessary. Although outsourcing firms might perform well on tests before they're hired, their actual production often falls short. Outsourcing firms recruit talented, experienced representatives for tests to win contracts. After the ink dries on the paper, outsourcing firms delegate the real production to interns and inexperienced staff.

Although you might encounter challenges with outsourcing partners, collaborate with them instead of complaining about them. (Okay, sometimes outsourced results are *really* bad.) Outsourcing is here to stay, and, especially in the art domain, outsourcing's popularity is growing.

The most prestigious studios don't rely solely on outsourcing. Instead, they plan effective designs, and they hire well-trained artists. Essentially, these studios accomplish more work using fewer employees. Investment in better production pipelines and employee tools contributes to these studios' success.

Despite the stigma, many studios instruct employees to revise and polish the outsourced contributions. Studios strategize using inadequate tools and inefficient pipelines, trying to stay within schedule. No wonder crunch is so rampant in the industry.

2   Evaluating Fields Similar to Game Development

When you search for opportunities, you might consider alternative career choices in fields similar to game development. For example, the film industry compares to the video game industry, but filmmakers are more competitive and participate in shorter projects. The film industry supports more freelance gigs than stable, full-time careers.

A professor with a knack for placing students into game studios revealed that the film industry is unpredictable and unstable. Employees move between studios after projects unless production companies produce multiple projects and keep people steadily employed. Historically, the game industry could do this. Recently, however, the game industry's volatility is growing.

The following additional careers resemble video game development:

- **Architecture:** Architecture is more stable than video games and requires fewer working hours per week. However, you might find architecture less fulfilling and creative, especially during the earlier years of an architecture career. It takes years to gain access to the more important work. A colleague who worked in architecture said that he spent days working on a design for a kitchen cabinet and handle, and the time crawled.

- **Military:** Military employment is secure and pays better than the game industry, but you might find it less invigorating.

- **Technology/Software Development:** Programming is the same for software and games. Employees in other software industries work regular hours, and some software industries are equally as creative as the game industry. Other programmers prefer avoiding life-or-death situations, opting to develop lighthearted games instead of advanced missile technology, for example.

3   Negotiating Sign-On Bonuses

Studios sometimes offer sign-on bonuses to experienced job candidates with expertise in the development styles of multiple studios—especially seniors. Don't request a sign-on bonus when you are new to the industry. Studios don't need to hire you that badly, especially when you lack a proven track record.

4   Differentiating Casual Versus Serious

Studios are casual about dress and personality, but they're serious about work ethic and attitude. They fire employees who exhibit casual attitudes about the work required to develop games. Managers wear jeans and t-shirts, and they don't always speak appropriately. Problems arise when regular developers confuse *casual dress* with a *casual work ethic*, thus missing deadlines or lacking attention to detail.

Without reading between the lines, you might miss what's underneath the surface. Hardworking developers are equally as professional as employees in other fields. Developers prefer to dress comfortably because they *can*. Developers rarely interact with the public, so they're less concerned about their office attire. You might encounter people who seem casual in their dress and personalities, but they're conscientious of their work ethic. Studios strive to hire more of these employees.

Goofing off is prevalent in the industry. Distractions require employees to contribute more when they approach deadlines. Some employees take two-hour lunch breaks and leave the office thirty minutes early, then complain during crunch.

Vacations are usually taken during slower periods, because—as mentioned earlier—studios encourage developers to take vacation after they meet deadlines. Developers are usually unmotivated and relax a little *too* much during these times, only to discover that tasks must get done eventually. That's why the tail end of a project is often the hardest. Working hard and smart from the beginning is the best strategy to prevent crunch.

5   Being the Best

If we can't be the best at what we do, then why do it at all? Shouldn't we choose better career paths so we could be the best?

Separate the tasks you enjoy from tasks that you are genetically and mentally compelled to do well. If you accept mediocrity, you have no place in the game industry. Game industry professionals are dedicated to their skills, and they constantly one-up each other.

If you like art, but your talents are more useful in design, then become a designer. You might stay mediocre forever doing something you're not meant to do. When you redirect your energy to maximize your natural abilities, you soar!

6   Balancing Personal Relationships

I included this section in the book because professionals I surveyed about relationships weren't much help. I haven't found an absolute solution for the problem. How do you maintain a relationship in the game industry? Aren't game industry professionals obligated to spend more time at the office than they spend with their significant others?

You might relocate fifteen hundred miles away to pursue a new opportunity. Your studio is crunching and your boyfriend or girlfriend wonders why you're ignoring him or her. You get funny looks from outsiders who don't understand creative industries. They suspect your employer exploits you, forcing you to toil seventy hours a week for six months straight without overtime pay.

That's reality in the game industry. Thankfully, I don't yet have a family to support. As the game industry matures, more game industry professionals consider supporting spouses and kids.

My girlfriend of three years dreams about her future career in a similar creative industry—acting. Most of our disagreements relate to my commitment to my vocation. Sometimes I neglect to spend enough time with her.

I now set aside weekends to spend time with her. Sometimes, I fear that single colleagues have nothing better to do than obsess over their projects, which might be an advantage to staying employed over someone who desires a well-balanced life.

It is difficult to maintain a relationship with someone outside the video game industry. Many people form relationships with others in the game industry for this reason. As the game industry becomes more incorporated in everyday society, it gets easier to maintain a relationship with people outside our circle. But, for now, connecting with people in similar fields makes it easier to avoid dysfunctional relationships.

7   Giving Back

A great way to maintain your skills is active participation in forums and mods. Online community members help each other improve their skills, and they match candidates with suitable job openings. Make a habit of doing the same for others, and stay active in the forums. Spread your knowledge, and help other aspiring video game professionals improve. Push the limits of possibilities in video games. The karma is well worth it.

CONCLUSION

doubt the game industry was ever *easy* to get into. Although there was less competition in the past, there was also less training, fewer opportunities, and few dedicated college programs. The skills required to produce the games of the past were more technical and harder to learn. Unintuitive tools required patience. Video games were new and unconquered territory.

Today, video games can simulate realistic experiences, approaching cinematic quality. The tools improve, developers get smarter, and studios grow bigger. Until fairly recently, video games were considered recession-proof. Studios close left and right, forcing developers into other industries and proving the fallacy of that belief.

The average length of game industry careers slowly increases. In the past, the industry considered five years to be extensive experience. Now, developers keep their jobs longer, bloating the already oversaturated industry. Throw outsourcing into the mix, and the grand scheme of a project implies that many people's livelihoods depend on the success of a single game.

Getting a job in the game industry doesn't require only skill or passion for games. Game studios want to hire conscientious and charismatic candidates who collaborate well with others. As the game industry grows more competitive, the bar rises higher for newcomers. Only the few great thrive. When you adapt, learn the latest software, and follow development pipelines, you rise above the rest. With increasing popularity of casual and social media games, the industry grows to reach a larger market of video game players. Most cultures widely accept video games as a leisurely pastime—commensurate to watching television. Successful developers are propelled to stardom.

It's a great time to get into video games. You can do anything that you set your mind to doing. When you commit to getting a job in the video game industry and you constantly practice, learn, and focus on that goal, it becomes a reality.

INDEX

CPSIA information can be obtained at www.ICGtesting.com
Printed in the USA
BVOW05s0359090715

407826BV00028B/979/P